"This beautiful book will brush the dust from your dingy days and reveal the extraordinary that is to be found in the ordinary. No mundane daily task will be the same once these pages open your eyes to how the work of your hands reflects the ways of the Creator and the rhythms of eternity."

Karen Swallow Prior, author of *Booked* and *Fierce Convictions*

"In this moment in culture, when much feels complicated and shallow, Tish Harrison Warren offers a beautiful and life-giving narrative: a way toward the ordinary sacred. This book is gentle in its simplicity and rich in wisdom. I wish I had read it a decade ago."

Micha Boyett, author of *Found*

"If Christianity is to retain its witness in our frenetic and fragmented age, it must take root not only in the thoughts and emotions but also in the daily lives and even bodies of those who call Christ Lord. Tish Harrison Warren has beautifully 'enfleshed' the concepts and doctrines of our faith into quotidian moments, showing how every hour of each day can become an occasion of grace and renewal. If you want to know how faith matters amid messy kitchens, unfinished manuscripts, marital spats, and unmade beds, *Liturgy of the Ordinary* will train your eyes to see holy beauty all around."

Katelyn Beaty, print managing editor, *Christianity Today*

"Sometimes the difference between drudgery and epiphany is just seeing things from the right angle, a frame that reframes everything, even the mundane. This marvelous little book is that certain slant of light that illuminates the everyday as an arena of sanctification, where the Spirit makes us holy in ways we might miss. You don't need more to do in a day, Warren shows. Instead, reframe the everyday as an extension of worship, and folding the laundry, washing dishes, and even commuting become habitations of the Spirit."

James K. A. Smith, author of *Desiring the Kingdom* and *You Are What You Love*

"Tish Harrison Warren shows us what it looks like to be . . . shaped and formed, in a book as down-to-earth and inviting as it is wise. I don't know of any book that's more winsome in commending a life lived in sync with the church calendar."

Wesley Hill, assistant professor of biblical studies,
Trinity School for Ministry, Ambridge, Pennsylvania

"Big gifts often come in small packages—sometimes even a plain cardboard box. Tish Harrison Warren has a talent for unpacking these gifts that God has placed all around us."

Michael Horton, professor of theology, Westminster Seminary California, author of *Ordinary*

"God's life and kingdom surround us on every side. But how do we find this reality and derive our life from God's—like a branch does from the vine? In *Liturgy of the Ordinary*, Tish Harrison Warren reveals simple, grounded, and beautifully repetitive practices in the small things of our workaday lives and the rhythms of liturgy. Tish gets it. If you let her be your guide, you too will get it: a life in God in your everyday life."

Todd Hunter, bishop, Anglican Church in North America, author of *Giving Church Another Chance*

"*Liturgy of the Ordinary* is a baptism of vision. Tish Harrison Warren warmly and wisely helps us find God in the strangest of places: standing at the sink, sitting in traffic, stooping to make a bed. As it turns out, our everyday habits are imbued with the holy possibility of becoming new people in Christ."

Jen Pollock Michel, author of *Teach Us to Want*

"Tish Harrison Warren is both a priest and a mother who changes poopy diapers. She embodies the high calling of the church and the high calling of the home and in those dual vocations has written a book of tremendous importance. . . . Tish writes with candor, insight, and intelligence about the sacredness of quotidian living. The highest compliment I can offer is that her book inspired me to go back to my dirty sink and my screaming kids with a renewed sense of purpose."

Andrea Palpant Dilley, contributing editor, *Christianity Today*

"Sunday liturgy shapes our faith through its mix of prayers, songs, Scriptures, and sermons. We hear from and are shaped by God through these practices. Under Tish Harrison Warren's insightful gaze, our seemingly 'boring' daily routines become a liturgy of their own—calling us to confession and community, Scripture and Sabbath, baptism and embodiment. Some spiritual directors listen for God's invitations in our prayers. Tish discerns God's invitations in our everyday life. She reminds us that God intends to speak, to invite, and to transform us in every situation we find ourselves in. Tish confronts us with the reality that God will not be confined to 1.5 hours on a Sunday. She is the prophet and pastor that our churches desperately need. At least this harried working dad needs her voice. I am approaching the daily routines of housework and homemaking with my wife and kids with newfound expectation and hope."

Gregory Jao, vice president and director of campus engagement, InterVarsity Christian Fellowship

To Arlene
May CRHP3 grow
together in faith and love

Mary

Dec 2022

liturgy of
the ordinary

sacred practices
in everyday life

Tish Harrison Warren
Foreword by Andy Crouch

An imprint of InterVarsity Press
Downers Grove, Illinois

InterVarsity Press
P.O. Box 1400, Downers Grove, IL 60515-1426
ivpress.com
email@ivpress.com

InterVarsity Press® is the book-publishing division of InterVarsity Christian Fellowship/USA®, a movement of students and faculty active on campus at hundreds of universities, colleges, and schools of nursing in the United States of America, and a member movement of the International Fellowship of Evangelical Students. For information about local and regional activities, visit intervarsity.org.

Scripture quotations, unless otherwise noted, are from The Holy Bible, English Standard Version, copyright © 2001 by Crossway Bibles, a division of Good News Publishers. Used by permission. All rights reserved.

While any stories in this book are true, some names and identifying information may have been changed to protect the privacy of individuals.

Cover design: Cindy Kiple
Interior design: Daniel van Loon
Images: peanut butter on bread: © Don Nichols/iStockphoto
  jelly on bread: © Don Nichols/iStockphoto

ISBN 978-0-8308-4678-8 (casebound)
ISBN 978-0-8308-4623-8 (paperback)
ISBN 978-0-8308-9220-4 (digital)

Printed in the United States of America ∞

InterVarsity Press is committed to ecological stewardship and to the conservation of natural resources in all our operations. This book was printed using sustainably sourced paper.

Library of Congress Cataloging-in-Publication Data
Names: Harrison Warren, Tish, 1979- author.
Title: Liturgy of the ordinary : sacred practices in everyday life / Tish Harrison Warren.
Description: Downers Grove : InterVarsity Press, 2016. | Includes bibliographical references.
Identifiers: LCCN 2016041776 (print) | LCCN 2016044733 (ebook) | ISBN 9780830846238
  (pbk. : alk. paper) | ISBN 9780830892204 (eBook)
Subjects: LCSH: God—Worship and love. | Worship. | Christian life.
Classification: LCC BV4817 .H373 2016 (print) | LCC BV4817 (ebook) | DDC 248.3—dc23
LC record available at https://lccn.loc.gov/2016041776

P 23 22 21 20 19 18 17 16 15 14 13 12 11 10 9 8 7 6 5 4 3 2 1

Y 37 36 35 34 33 32 31 30 29 28 27 26 25 24 23 22 21 20 19

To Jonathan

My love, my friend—how was your day?

contents

foreword
andy crouch

The structure of this book is simple, with a touch of genius.

It encompasses one day, from our very first moments of waking in the morning on the first page to our drifting off into sleep on the last. No more and no less. But in between, with the writer's (and indeed the poet's) gift of slowing down and paying the best kind of attention, Tish Harrison Warren connects the moments of an ordinary day with the extraordinary pattern of classical Christian worship.

In doing so, Tish dismantles that most stubborn of Christian heresies: the idea that there is any part of our lives that is secular, untouched by and disconnected from the real sacred work of worship and prayer. This misreading of the human condition has taken many forms over the centuries, even though it should have been dealt a decisive blow by Jesus' earthly, earthy life as Son of Man and Son of God. It takes many forms in our time—some easier to recognize than others. There is our tendency to speak of the sanctuary as somehow of more importance to God than the workplace or the home, and those (like Tish) specially ordained to its work as somehow closer to God than those who work in the convenience store or the office complex.

But there is also the more subtle quest for a suitably "radical" life, a life of conspicuous sacrifice and service—a life that seems obviously set apart for something more than the mundane and (so we start to think) unimportant life. In this version of the ancient error, nonprofit work is more spiritual than for-profit work; urban neighborhoods are more spiritual than suburban ones; bicycles are more spiritual than minivans.

As someone who is both ordained to priestly service and who has invested her life in radical ways to serve the materially and spiritually poor, Tish is the perfect person to help us discover just how wrong-headed these sacred-secular distinctions are. Like all heresies, this one can only be conquered by the beauty of orthodoxy, and the beautiful orthodoxy that undermines all our foolish secularizing is that endlessly surprising Christian doctrine, the incarnation. The Word became flesh. The Word went fishing. The Word slept. The Word woke up with morning breath. The Word brushed his teeth—or at least he would have, if the Word had been a twenty-first-century American instead of a first-century Judean. This uniquely Christian belief is amazing, faintly horrifying, and life-changing.

And just as wonderfully, the genius of this book is to show us that the dismantling goes in the other direction as well. In Tish's telling, and in any honest Christian's experience, the sacred liturgy itself is as ordinary as can be much of the time. We say the same prayers, make the same gestures, arrive and leave in one sense much the same people we were the previous Sunday, and the Sunday to come. (And this is just as true, of course, of Christians who worship in nonliturgical churches!)

It is not just that the secular is shot through with the sacred. Worship itself is made up of ordinary stuff. We use plain words.

Some of the most the glorious words in Cranmer's *Book of Common Prayer* are, well, common and plain enough to make you weep—"We have left undone those things which we ought to have done, and we have done those things which we ought not to have done, and there is no health in us." We are baptized in plain water. We consume plain bread and wine. And it all is lifted up by plain people.

Yet all of this is far from ordinary. Our bodies, our pleasures, our fears, our fatigue, our friendships, our fights—these are in fact the stuff of our formation and transformation into the frail but infinitely dignified creatures we were meant to be and shall become. Our moments of exaltation and our stifled yawns—somehow they go together, part of the whole life that we are meant to offer to God day by day, as well as Sunday by Sunday, the life that God has taken into his own life. It is the life that Christ himself assumed, and thus rescued and redeemed.

With its laugh-out-loud moments and moving descriptions of a life lived imperfectly but well, this is a great gift of a book—an ordinary book, in one way, but also not ordinary at all. Take and read. Taste—not just the wine and bread, but the peanut butter and jelly, too—and see. The Lord is good. Every square inch of our lives, every second, is his.

It must be remembered that life consists not of a series of illustrious actions, or elegant enjoyments; the greater part of our time passes in compliance with necessities, in the performance of daily duties, in the removal of small inconveniences, in the procurement of petty pleasures.

DR. JOHNSON

It is a quotidian mystery that dailiness can lead to such despair and yet also be at the core of our salvation. . . . We want life to have meaning, we want fulfillment, healing and even ecstasy, but the human paradox is that we find these things by starting where we are. . . . We must look for blessings to come from unlikely, everyday places.

KATHLEEN NORRIS

That we ought not to be weary of doing little things for the love of God, who regards not the greatness of the work, but the love with which it is performed. That we should not wonder if, in the beginning, we often failed in our endeavors, but that at last we should gain a habit, which will naturally produce its acts in us, without our care, and to our exceeding great delight.

BROTHER LAWRENCE

1

waking

baptism and learning to be beloved

I wake slowly. Even when the day demands I rally quickly—when my kids leap on top of me with sharp elbows or my alarm blares— I lie still for the first few seconds of the day, stunned, orienting, thoughts dulled. Then comes, slowly, the dawning of plans to make and goals for the day. But in those first delicate seconds, the bleary-eyed pause of waking, before the tasks begin, before I get on my game, I'm greeted again with the truth of who I am in my most basic self.

Whether we're children or heads of state, we sit in our pajamas for a moment, yawning, with messy hair and bad breath, un-productive, groping toward the day. Soon we'll get buttoned up into our identities: mothers, business people, students, friends, citizens. We'll spend our day conservative or liberal, rich or poor, earnest or cynical, fun-loving or serious. But as we first emerge from sleep, we are nothing but human, unimpressive, vulnerable, newly born into the day, blinking as our pupils adjust to light and our brains emerge into consciousness.

I always try to stay in bed longer. My body is greedy for sleep—"Just a few more minutes!"

But it's not just sleep I'm greedy for—it's that in-between place, liminal consciousness, where I'm cozy, not quite alert to the demands that await me. I don't want to face the warring, big and small, that lies ahead of me today. I don't want to don an identity yet. I want to stay in the womb of my covers a little longer.

◆ ◆ ◆

It's remarkable that when the Father declares at Jesus' baptism, "This is my beloved Son, with whom I am well pleased," Jesus hasn't yet done much of anything that many would find impressive. He hasn't yet healed anyone or resisted Satan in the wilderness. He hasn't yet been crucified or resurrected. It would make more sense if the Father's proud announcement came after something grand and glorious—the triumphant moment after feeding a multitude or the big reveal after Lazarus is raised.

But after hearing about Jesus' birth and a brief story about his boyhood, we find him again as a grown man at the banks of the Jordan. He's one in a crowd, squinting in the sun, sand gritty between his toes.

The one who is worthy of worship, glory, and fanfare spent decades in obscurity and ordinariness. As if the incarnation itself is not mind-bending enough, the incarnate God spent his days quietly, a man who went to work, got sleepy, and lived a pedestrian life among average people.

Jesus emerges from water a commoner, wet and messy haired. And suddenly the Spirit of God shows up and the deep mystery of the universe reverberates through the air: this is the Son of God, the Son the Father loves, in whom he is pleased.

Jesus is sent first to the desert and then into his public ministry. But he is sent out with a declaration of the Father's love.

Jesus is eternally beloved by the Father. His every activity unfurls from his identity as the Beloved. He loved others, healed others, preached, taught, rebuked, and redeemed not in order to gain the Father's approval, but out of his rooted certainty in the Father's love.

◆ ◆ ◆

Baptism is the first word of grace spoken over us by the church.

In my tradition, Anglicanism, we baptize infants. Before they cognitively understand the story of Christ, before they can affirm a creed, before they can sit up, use the bathroom, or contribute significantly to the work of the church, grace is spoken over them and they are accepted as part of us. They are counted as God's people before they have anything to show for themselves.

When my daughters were baptized, we had a big celebration with cupcakes and champagne. Together with our community we sang "Jesus Loves Me" over the newly baptized. It was a proclamation: before you know it, before you doubt it, before you confess it, before you can sing it yourself, you are beloved by God, not by your effort but because of what Christ has done on your behalf. We are weak, but he is strong.

In many liturgical churches baptismal fonts are situated at the back of the sanctuary. As people walk into church to worship, they pass by it. This symbolizes how baptism is the entrance into the people of God. It reminds us that before we begin to worship— before we even sit down in church—we are marked as people who belong to Jesus by grace alone, swept up into good news, which we received as a gift from God and from believers who went before us.

As worshipers enter the sanctuary and pass the font, they dip their fingers in it and make the sign of the cross. They do this as an act of recollection—remembering their own baptism and recalling that they are loved and approved of because of Jesus' work. When my eldest daughter was very young, barely able to walk, I'd lift her up to the baptismal font at the entrance of our sanctuary and let her touch the water. I'd whisper, "Remember your baptism." She didn't yet know the words of the liturgy or the theology of sacraments but this visceral experience—the hard basin of the font, the cool water on her fingers—was her entrance into worship.

According to Lutheran theologian Martin Marty, Lutherans are taught to begin each day, first thing, by making the sign of the cross as a token of their baptism.[1] Dorothy Bass explains this practice: "For all Christians, baptism embodies release from yesterday's sin and receipt of tomorrow's promise: going under the water, the old self is buried in the death of Christ; rising from the water the self is new, joined to the resurrected Christ." Martin Luther charged each member of his community to regard baptism "as the daily garment which he is to wear all the time."[2]

We enter each new day as we enter the sanctuary, by remembering our baptism. Each morning Marty crosses himself—what he calls his "non-verbal prayer." He remembers again that he is forgiven for all that has come before and that there will be grace enough for all that lies ahead.[3]

I was baptized in a little Baptist church in a small town in Texas when I was about six years old. I don't remember much about it. I remember—at least I think I remember—the odd feeling of my long robe billowing in warm water; I remember enjoying all the hugging and attention from grownups afterward, and being thrilled that I could now drink grape juice in church; and I remember the photographs I've seen in an old album of a tiny me with wet hair and a squinty smile in front of a short brick building with a steeple.

We are marked from our first waking moment
by an identity that is given to us by grace:
an identity that is deeper and more real than
any other identity we will don that day.

But by "remembering our baptism," I do not mean that we must literally recall historic details of an event in our life, which I personally can barely remember. Instead, I recall that one Sunday morning, as I was plunged under water "in the name of the Father, Son, and Holy Spirit," I was marked. In the Anglican baptismal liturgy, we tell the newly baptized that they are "sealed by the Holy Spirit in baptism and marked as Christ's own for ever." Galatians tells us that we are clothed in Christ in baptism (Gal 3:27), clothed in the Beloved Son in whom the Father is well pleased. To use Paul's more chilling image, on that day as a six-year-old, I died and was buried, and then, reversing the whole order of the universe, newly born with Christ (Rom 6:3-5).

As Christians, we wake each morning as those who are baptized. We are united with Christ and the approval of the Father is spoken over us. We are marked from our first waking moment by an identity that is given to us by grace: an identity that is deeper and more real than any other identity we will don that day.

My wet fingers dipped in the baptismal font remind me that everything I do in the liturgy—all the confessing and singing, kneeling and peace passing, distraction, boredom, ecstasy, devotion—is a response to God's work and God's initiation. And before we begin the liturgies of our day—the cooking, sitting in traffic, emailing, accomplishing, working, resting—we begin beloved. My works and worship don't earn a thing. Instead, they flow from God's love, gift, and work on my behalf. I am not primarily defined by my abilities or marital status or how I vote or my successes or failures or fame or obscurity, but as one who is sealed in the Holy Spirit, hidden in Christ, and beloved by the Father. My naked self is one who is baptized.

This reality seeps out of my soul quickly. Days can pass in a bluster of busyness, impatience, and distraction. I work to build my own blessedness, to strive for a self-made belovedness. But each morning in those first tender moments—in simply being God's smelly, sleepy beloved—I again receive grace, life, and faith as a gift. Grace is a mystery and the joyful scandal of the universe.

In this book we look at practices—how we spend our days, how we worship together. But before we begin we must note that though these rituals and habits may form us as an alternative people marked by the love and new life of Jesus, they are not what make us beloved. The reality underlying every practice in our life is the triune God and his story, mercy, abundance, generosity, initiative, and pleasure.

◅◆▻

This morning I wake (slowly) on an ordinary day, a cool morning in mid-March. I do not know what lies ahead, but I wake in a bed I know, a house I live in, a routine, a particular life, in medias res.

The psalmist declares, "This is the day that the Lord has made." This one. We wake not to a vague or general mercy from a far-off God. God, in delight and wisdom, has made, named, and blessed this average day. What I in my weakness see as another monotonous day in a string of days, God has given as a singular gift.

When Jesus died for his people, he knew me by name in the particularity of this day. Christ didn't redeem my life theoretically or abstractly—the life I dreamed of living or the life I think I ideally should be living. He knew I'd be in today as it is, in my home where it stands, in my relationships with their specific beauty and brokenness, in my particular sins and struggles.

> **God is forming us into a new people.**
> **And the place of that formation is**
> **in the small moments of today.**

In *The Divine Conspiracy*, Dallas Willard reminds us that where "transformation is actually carried out is in our real life, where we dwell with God and our neighbors. . . . First, we must accept the circumstances we constantly find ourselves in as the place of God's kingdom and blessing. God has yet to bless anyone except where they actually are."[4]

The new life into which we are baptized is lived out in days, hours, and minutes. God is forming us into a new people. And the place of that formation is in the small moments of today.

Alfred Hitchcock said movies are "life with the dull bits cut out."[5] Car chases and first kisses, interesting plot lines and good conversations. We don't want to watch our lead character going on a walk, stuck in traffic, or brushing his teeth—at least not for long, and not without a good soundtrack.

We tend to want a Christian life with the dull bits cut out.

Yet God made us to spend our days in rest, work, and play, taking care of our bodies, our families, our neighborhoods, our homes. What if all these boring parts matter to God? What if days passed in ways that feel small and insignificant to us are weighty with meaning and part of the abundant life that God has for us?

◆ ◆ ◆

Christ's ordinary years are part of our redemption story. Because of the incarnation and those long, unrecorded years of Jesus' life, our small, normal lives matter. If Christ was a carpenter, all of us who are in Christ find that our work is sanctified and made holy. If Christ spent time in obscurity, then there is infinite worth found in obscurity. If Christ spent most of his life in quotidian ways, then all of life is brought under his lordship. There is no task too small or too routine to reflect God's glory and worth.

I have a friend who was a missionary in Calcutta among the poorest of the poor. He told me that what struck him was how mundane life was even in such a foreign and challenging place. His decision to go overseas felt daring and bold, but he was surprised to find that wherever he was on earth, much of his day was spent sitting with people, taking care of business and chores, taking care of his own body, knowing his neighbors, seeking to love people—sometimes succeeding, sometimes failing. Whether you're Mother Teresa or a stay-at-home mom, whether you're a revolutionary, a student, or a tax attorney, life is lived in twenty-four-hour days. We have bodies; we lag in energy; we learn slowly; we wake daily and don't know what lies ahead.

In these pages we look at life in one day. We look at faith in small moments, spiritual formation in its molecular form—not because this is all that matters, but because the only life any of us live is in daily, pedestrian humanity.

I like big ideas. I can get drunk on talk of justification, ecclesiology, pneumatology, Christology, and eschatology. But these big ideas are borne out—lived, believed, and enfleshed—in the small moments of our day, in the places, seasons, homes, and communities that compose our lives. Annie Dillard famously writes, "How we spend our days is, of course, how we spend our lives."[6] I came across Dillard's words a couple years before I went to seminary, and throughout those years of heady theological study I kept them in my back pocket. They remind me that today is the proving ground of what I believe and of whom I worship.

And every new day, this is the turn my heart must make: I'm living this life, the life right in front of me. This one where marriages struggle. This one where we aren't living as we thought we might or as we hoped we would. This one where we are weary, where we want to make a difference but aren't sure where to start, where we have to get dinner on the table or the kids' teeth brushed, where we have back pain and boring weeks, where our lives look small, where we doubt, where we wrestle with meaninglessness, where we worry about those we love, where we struggle to meet our neighbors and love those closest to us, where we grieve, where we wait.

And on this particular day, Jesus knows me and declares me his own. On this day he is redeeming the world, advancing his kingdom, calling us to repent and grow, teaching his church to worship, drawing near to us, and making a people all his own.

If I am to spend my whole life being transformed by the good news of Jesus, I must learn how grand, sweeping truths—doctrine, theology, ecclesiology, Christology—rub against the texture of an average day. How I spend this ordinary day in Christ is how I will spend my Christian life.

2

making the bed

liturgy, ritual, and what forms a life

A few years ago, right before Lent, I became curious about bed making. Specifically, it occurred to me that thousands, perhaps even millions, of adults make their beds—a shocking idea to me, because I almost never did.

I had assumed that most people, outside of a small group of elite Pinterest-perfect superhumans, didn't make their beds unless they were hosting a party or their mom was visiting. I know that for bed-making devotees this is hard to fathom, but in my mind bed making was something we all collectively shed as soon as we could, like wearing a retainer or doing algebra homework.

What was the point? You'd mess it up again that evening. It is a Sisyphean exercise. Make the bed, unmake it, make it again, over and over. And for what? The dishes must be washed so you can reuse them; the laundry must be done so you have clean clothes (although I stretch that as far as I can). But the bed functions just as well with the sheets messy as it does with them pulled tight and tucked in neatly. Don't get me wrong—I enjoyed the feeling of crawling into a made bed, especially with freshly cleaned sheets, but not so much that I actually considered making it.

Out of my newfound curiosity, I asked a close friend whether she made her bed. She did. Not daily, but more often than not, and funnily enough she usually did it in the evening, right before she crawled in. Well, that made no sense and totally intrigued me. So I took to Facebook and did an informal survey, asking who made their bed and how often. People responded—lots of people—with surprising passion.

Some made it daily, first thing, zealously. Some never made it. Some thought it was preposterous to even consider making it, while others thought not making the bed was akin to not brushing your teeth or not paying your taxes—something meriting disgust, if not jail time. Many made their bed erratically, maybe three out of seven days. A shocking number made their bed at night. Some promised me that bed making would change my life—that'd I'd be more successful, happy, and productive with a made bed.

◆ ◆ ◆

At that time, my typical morning routine was that shortly after waking, I'd grab my smartphone. Like digital caffeine, it would prod my foggy brain into coherence and activity. Before getting out of bed, I'd check my email, scroll through the news, glance at Facebook or Twitter.

If humans rescue a baby animal in the wild, the animal is said to be "imprinted." It accepts the human as its mother. From that point on, it will believe that all good things come from people. It is no longer wild and it cannot live on its own. The nature center in my town houses imprinted animals—baby mountain lions, raccoons, and porcupines who rely on humans for food, water, shelter, and protection.

My morning smartphone ritual was brief—no more than five or ten minutes. But I was imprinted. My day was imprinted by technology. And like a mountain lion cub attached to her humans, I'd look for all good things to come from glowing screens.

Without realizing it, I had slowly built a habit: a steady resistance to and dread of boredom.

Technology began to fill every empty moment in the day. Just before breakfast, I'd quickly scroll through email, Facebook, Twitter, a blog. And then again an hour later. I'd ignore my kids' persistent calls for milk and snacks with a distracted "hold on" as I vaguely skimmed an article. I'd sneak in five minutes online as they ate lunch. I'd return from an errand and sit in the driveway with the car running, scrolling through news on my phone, and then I'd check my screen again before bedtime. Throughout the day I fed on a near-constant stream of news, entertainment, stimulation, likes, and retweets. Without realizing it, I had slowly built a habit: a steady resistance to and dread of boredom.

◆◆◆

After my makeshift sociological study on bed making, I decided that for Lent that year I'd exchange routines: I'd stop waking up with my phone, and instead I'd make the bed, first thing. I also decided to spend the first few minutes after I made the bed sitting (on my freshly made bed) in silence. So I banished my smartphone from the bedroom.

My new Lenten routine didn't make me wildly successful or cheerfully buoyant as some had promised, but I began to notice, very subtly, that my day was imprinted differently. The first activity of my day, the first move I made, was not that of a consumer, but that of a colaborer with God. Instead of going to a device for a morning fix of instant infotainment, I touched the tangible softness of our well-worn covers, tugged against wrinkled cotton, felt the hard wood beneath my bare feet. In the creation story, God entered chaos and made order and beauty. In making my bed I reflected that creative act in the tiniest, most ordinary way. In my small chaos, I made small order.

And then there was a little space, an ordered rectangle in my messy home. And that rectangle somehow carved out a small ordered space in my messy, distracted mind.

And I sat. At times, I'd read Scripture. Most often I'd pray. I'd begin with the Lord's Prayer. Then I'd invite God into the day. I'd pray the words of the Morning Office: "Open my lips, O Lord, and my mouth shall declare your praise . . ."[1]

I'd lay out my worries, my hopes, and my questions before God, spreading them out in his presence like stretched-out sheets. I'd pray for my work and family, for decisions, for a meeting scheduled later in the day. But mostly, I'd invite God into the day and just sit. Silent. Sort of listening. Sort of just sitting.

But I sat expectantly. God made this day. He wrote it and named it and has a purpose in it. Today, he is the maker and giver of all good things. I'd lap up the silence like mother's milk.

——◆◆——

Most of our days, and therefore most of our lives, are driven by habit and routine.

Our way of being-in-the-world works its way into us through ritual and repetition. James K. A. Smith explains that a particular view of "the good life" is ingrained in us through repetitive practices that motivate how we live and what we love.[2]

We are shaped every day, whether we know it or not, by practices—rituals and liturgies that make us who we are. We receive these practices—which are often rote—not only from the church or the Scriptures but from the culture, from the "air around us."

Flannery O'Connor once told a young friend to "push as hard as the age that pushes against you."[3] The church is to be a radically alternative people, marked by the love of the triune God in each area of life. But often we are not sure how to become this sort of alternative people. Though we believe deeply in the gospel, though we put our hope in the resurrection, we often feel like the way we spend our days looks very similar to our unbelieving neighbors—with perhaps a bit of extra spirituality thrown in.

Some Christians seem to think that we push back against the age primarily by believing correctly—by getting the right ideas in our heads or having a biblical worldview. While doctrinal orthodoxy is crucial in the Christian life, for the most part we are not primarily motivated by our conscious thoughts. Most of what we do is precognitive.[4] We do not usually think about our beliefs or worldview as we brush our teeth, go grocery shopping, and drive our cars. Most of what shapes our life and culture works "below the mind"—in our gut, in our loves.[5]

Other Christians have believed that pushing against the age involves a radical rejection of the workaday world. If we can sufficiently separate ourselves from culture, the thinking goes, either by withdrawing from it and rejecting certain sorts of art, music, media, and parts of civic life or, alternatively, by a kind of Christian radicalism—living in alternative communities, forsaking average careers, going overseas, or intentionally living among the poor—then we will be formed as an alternative people. Though each of these approaches has valuable insight to offer about how to follow Christ in our contemporary culture, they are not enough to form an alternative people in themselves. They teach us to inhabit a specific subculture, rejecting the dominant culture by consuming our own sorts of music, conferences, books, media, celebrities, and lifestyles. While these approaches may form us as alternative consumers, they do not necessarily form us as worshipers.

Whoever we are, whatever we believe, wherever we live, and whatever our consumer preferences may be, we spend our days doing things—we live in routines formed by habits and practices. Smith, following Augustine, argues that to be an alternative people is to be formed differently—to take up practices and habits that aim our love and desire toward God.

We don't wake up daily and form a way of being-in-the-world from scratch, and we don't think our way through every action of our day. We move in patterns that we have set over time, day by day. These habits and practices shape our loves, our desires, and ultimately who we are and what we worship.

◆ ◆ ◆

In church on Sunday we participate in a liturgy—a ritualized way of worship—that we repeat each week and by which we are transformed. Our Sunday liturgies look different from tradition to tradition. Quakers, Roman Catholics, and Presbyterians worship differently, but within each tradition there are patterns of worship, and through each gathered liturgy congregants are formed in a way of being-in-the-world. Even those traditions that claim to be freeform or nonliturgical include practices and patterns in worship. Therefore, the question is not whether we have a liturgy. The question is, "What kind of people is our liturgy forming us to be?"

Our Sunday liturgies teach us a particular idea of the good life, and we are sent out into our week as people who bear out that vision in our workaday world.

There is nothing magic about any particular church tradition. Liturgy is never a silver bullet for sinfulness. These "formative practices" have no value outside of the gospel and God's own initiative and power.[6] But God has loved us and sought us—not only as individuals, but corporately as a people over millennia. As we learn the words, practices, and rhythms of faith hewn by our brothers and sisters throughout history, we learn to live our days in worship.

We have everyday habits—formative practices—that constitute daily liturgies. By reaching for my smartphone every morning, I had developed a ritual that trained me toward a certain end: entertainment and stimulation via technology. Regardless of my professed worldview or particular Christian subculture, my unexamined daily habit was shaping me into a worshiper of glowing screens.

Examining my daily liturgy *as a liturgy*—as something that both revealed and shaped what I love and worship—allowed me to realize that my daily practices were malforming me, making me less alive, less human, less able to give and receive love throughout my day. Changing this ritual allowed me to form a new repetitive and contemplative habit that pointed me toward a different way of being-in-the-world.

Smith asks us to examine our days:

So the question is, are there habits and practices that we acquire without knowing it? Are there ritual forces in our culture that we perhaps naively immerse ourselves in—and are thus formed by—that, when we consider them more closely, are pointed at some ultimate end? Are there mundane routines that we participate in that, if we are attentive, function as thick practices aimed at a particular vision of the good life?[7]

The often unseen and unsung ways we spend our time are what form us. Our mundane moments, rooted in the communal practices of the church, shape us through habit and repetition, moment by passing moment, into people who spend their days and therefore their lives marked by the love of God.

As we walk together through an average day, we will look at these common, often overlooked daily practices as liturgies of the day, liturgies that are utterly intertwined with and transformed by our communal liturgies each Sunday. Some of these, like my smartphone ritual, may need to be changed. As we examine them we realize that we need to make new habits that form us as more faithful worshipers. Some habits may simply need to be examined as the important spiritual practices they are.

I do not expect that as we navigate our day we will consciously think through the theology of each and every habit. That would be exhausting. But whether we examine our daily activities theologically or not, they shape our view of God and ourselves. Examining our daily life through the lens of liturgy allows us to see who these habits are shaping us to be, and the ways we can live as people who have been loved and transformed by God.

◆ ◆ ◆

My Lenten ritual of making the bed each day and sitting cross-legged in a silent room was a practice that reacquainted me with the texture of silence and the rhythm of repetition. I need rituals that encourage me to embrace what is repetitive, ancient, and quiet.

But what I crave is novelty and stimulation.

And I am not alone. A fascinating and somewhat disturbing study out of the University of Virginia showed that, given the choice, many preferred undergoing electric shock to sitting alone with their thoughts. Study participants were exposed to a mild shock, which they all reported they didn't like and would pay money not to undergo again. But when left alone in an empty room with a "shocker" button for up to fifteen minutes, removed from all distractions, unable to check their phones or listen to music, two-thirds of men and one-fourth of women in the study chose to voluntarily shock themselves rather than sit in silence. Dr. Tim Wilson, who helped conduct the study, said, "I think this could be why, for many of us, external activities are so appealing, even at the level of the ubiquitous cell phone that so many of us keep consulting. . . . The mind is so prone to want to engage with the world, it will take any opportunity to do so."[8]

The thing that most annoyed me about bed making—the fact that it must be done over and over again—reflects the very rhythm of faith. Our hearts and our loves are shaped by what we do again and again and again. On Sunday in gathered worship, we learn together to sit in repetition and in predictability. We learn the repetitive, slow rhythms of a life of faith.

My Lenten bed making ritual—which has continued for years and is now ingrained—teaches me to slow down, to bravely enter a dull Tuesday morning, to embrace daily life, believing that in these small moments God meets us and brings meaning to our average day. We are not left like Sisyphus, cursed by the gods to a life of meaninglessness, repeating the same pointless task for eternity. Instead, these small bits of our day are profoundly meaningful because they are the site of our worship. The crucible of our formation is in the monotony of our daily routines.

In a culture that craves the big, the entertaining, the dramatic, and the shocking (sometimes literally), cultivating a life with space for silence and repetition is necessary for sustaining a life of faith.

While my husband, Jonathan, was getting his PhD, he got to know a former Jesuit priest turned married professor—a holy man, a provocateur, and a favorite among his students. Once a student met with him to complain about having to read Augustine's *Confessions*. "It's boring," the student whined. "No, it's not boring," the professor responded. "You're boring."

What Jonathan's professor meant is that when we gaze at the richness of the gospel and the church and find them dull and uninteresting, it's actually we who have been hollowed out. We have lost our capacity to see wonders where true wonders lie. We must be formed as people who are capable of appreciating goodness, truth, and beauty.

The crucible of our formation is in the anonymous monotony of our daily routines.

Our worship together as a church forms us in a particular way. We must be shaped into people who value that which gives life, not just what's trendy or loud or exciting. I worry that when our gathered worship looks like a rock show or an entertainment special, we are being formed as consumers—people after a thrill and a rush—when what we need is to learn a way of being-in-the-world that transforms us, day by day, by the rhythms of repentance and faith. We need to learn the slow habits of loving God and those around us.

Our addiction to stimulation, input, and entertainment empties us out and makes us boring—unable to embrace the ordinary wonders of life in Christ. Kathleen Norris writes,

> Like liturgy, the work of cleaning draws much of its meaning and value from repetition, from the fact that it is never completed, but only set aside until the next day. Both liturgy and what is euphemistically termed "domestic" work also have an intense relation with the present moment, a kind of faith in the present that fosters hope and makes life seem possible in the day-to-day.[9]

Daily life, dishes in the sink, children that ask the same questions and want the same stories again and again and again, the long doldrums of the afternoon—these things are filled with repetition. And much of the Christian life is returning over and over to the same work and the same habits of worship. We must contend with the same spiritual struggles again and again. The work of repentance and faith is daily and repetitive. Again and again, we repent and believe.

A sign hangs on the wall in a New Monastic Christian community house: "Everyone wants a revolution. No one wants to do the dishes." I was, and remain, a Christian who longs for revolution, for things to be made new and whole in beautiful and big ways. But what I am slowly seeing is that you can't get to the revolution without learning to do the dishes. The kind of spiritual life and disciplines needed to sustain the Christian life are quiet, repetitive, and ordinary. I often want to skip the boring, daily stuff to get to the thrill of an edgy faith. But it's in the dailiness of the Christian faith—the making the bed, the doing the dishes, the praying for our enemies, the reading the Bible, the quiet, the small—that God's transformation takes root and grows.

❖❖❖

The point of my new morning practice was not to have a magazine-cover bedroom—which in my house, with my domestic and decorating skills, is never going to happen. The point is not that "cleanliness is next to godliness." There are times when we may need to leave the dishes in the sink and go for a walk or hang out with our friends or play with our kids or take a nap.

The point of exchanging my morning liturgy was to habituate myself to repetition, to the tangible, to the work before me—to train myself, in this tiny way, to live with my eyes open to God's presence in this ordinary day. I'd cultivated a habit, from the first conscious moments of my day, of being entertained, informed, and stimulated. My brain would dart quickly from stimulus to stimulus, unable to focus, unable to lie fallow. Making my bed and sitting in silence for just a few minutes reminded me that what is most real and significant in my day is not what is loudest, flashiest, or most entertaining. It is in the repetitive and the mundane that I begin to learn to love, to listen, to pay attention to God and to those around me.

I needed to retrain my mind not to bolt at the first sight of boredom or buck against stillness. That took the cultivation of habit. And habits have to start small and to start somewhere—sitting half bored to pray and to listen on sheets tucked in, covers pulled tight.

3

brushing teeth

standing, kneeling, bowing, and living in a body

So much of life, unavoidably, is just maintenance. Things need upkeep or they fall apart. We spend most of our days and much of our energy simply staving off inevitable entropy and decay.

This is especially true of our bodies.

Our lives are taken up with the care and maintenance of our bodies—we have to clean them, feed them, deal with their wastes, exercise them, and give them rest, again and again, every day. And that's when we are well and things are running smoothly. Even with all that care, our bodies eventually break down and we get sick, and require even more care. Having a body is a lot of work.

This morning, I brushed my teeth—a mindless habit ingrained in me since before I can remember. I do so morning and night almost every day. I say "almost" because, at times, the sheer necessity of daily teeth brushing leaves me feeling resentful and, like a defiant teenager, I rebel against the system. I do not like having to do anything every day. There are days, every six months or so, where I go to bed without brushing my teeth. Just to prove I can. Just to prove that I am not a slave to my molars. It's ridiculous and possibly a little unhinged. But the needs of my body are so relentless that they feel burdensome and demanding. Teeth. So needy.

Yet, of course, the relationship I have with my body is not just one of slavish caregiving. The pleasures I get from having a body are manifest. Warm water on my skin in the shower, the texture of a ripe apple, the feeling of my legs stretching on a long walk, the smell of garlic simmering in olive oil. So I brush my teeth morning and night (almost) every day, because I want to be able to crunch chips and eat tacos as long as God gives me breath.

◆ ◆ ◆

We can believe that the cumulative hours and years spent on the incessant care of our bodies are meaningless, an insignificant necessity on the way to the important parts of our day. But in orthodox Christianity, our bodies matter profoundly.

Christians are often accused of two wrong-headed views of the body. One is that we ignore the body in favor of a disembodied, spirits-floating-on-clouds spirituality. The other is that we are obsessed with bodies, focusing all our attention on policing sexual conduct and denigrating the body as a dirty source of evil. In certain communities at certain moments in history these accusations may have been legitimate. But the Christianity we find in Scripture values and honors the body.

At root, Christianity is a thoroughly embodied faith. We believe in the incarnation—Christ came in a body. And while he may not have brushed his teeth with a pink Colgate brush like mine, he spent his days in the same kind of bodily maintenance that we do. He slept. He ate. He groomed. He took naps, got his feet dirty and had them washed, and likely enjoyed a good, long dinner since he was derided by his more ascetic critics as a drunkard and a glutton.

In the Scriptures we find that the body is not incidental to our faith, but integral to our worship. We were made to be embodied—to experience life, pleasure, and limits in our bodies. When Jesus redeems us, that redemption occurs in our bodies. And when we die, we will not float away to heaven and leave our bodies behind but will experience the resurrection of our bodies. Christ himself appeared after his resurrection in a mysteriously changed-but-fleshy eating and drinking body. Even now, he remains in his body.

The biblical call to an embodied morality—to sexual purity, for instance, or moderation in food and drink—comes not out of a disdain for the body and its appetites, but out of the understanding that our bodies are central to our life in Christ. Our bodies and souls are inseparable, and therefore what we do with our bodies and what we do with our souls are always entwined.

It's no wonder that one of the first heresies passionately opposed by the apostles was Gnosticism, which shunned the embodied life to embrace a higher spiritual reality. In Gnosticism, teeth brushing and shower taking and nail clipping would simply be burdensome hindrances to the soul's pure engagement with the spiritual life. But in Christ, these bodily tasks are a response to God's creative goodness. These teeth I'm brushing, this body I'm bathing, these nails I'm clipping were made by a loving Creator who does not reject the human body. Instead he declared us—holistically—"very good." He himself took on flesh in order to redeem us in our bodies, and in so doing he redeemed embodiment itself.

◗◆◗

We find in Genesis that, after the fall, having a body comes with the inevitable experience of shame. Adam and Eve saw their nakedness and sought to cover it, to hide from God and each other. Embodiment, while often a source of pleasure and joy, can be embarrassing. There is something that feels undignified about having a body. I brush my teeth to keep from having bad breath. I have to spit and floss and pry popcorn kernels out of my gums.

We don't even like to mention the more embarrassing aspects of living in a body. And yet God entered all of it. He did not shrink back from Adam and Eve's shame. Instead, he covered it.

In the incarnation, God entered not just the beauty and wonder of embodiment but also its shame. Jesus had bad breath. He may have wet the bed. His nose may have been lumpy or his teeth crooked. He stank. He covered his nakedness.

But because of the embodied life, death, and resurrection of Christ, we who are in Christ are "clothed in Christ." The shame of embodiment—and ultimately the shame of sin—that Adam and Eve could not cover with fig leaves is resolved, permanently, in Christ himself.

Jewish faith, the soil from which Christianity sprang, is delightfully, at times shockingly, earthy and embodied. Observant Jews use a prayer called the Asher Yatzar, which they recite after using the bathroom.

> Blessed are You, Hashem our God, King of the universe, Who formed man with wisdom and created within him many openings and many hollows. It is obvious and known before Your Throne of

Glory that if even one of them ruptures, or if even one of them becomes blocked, it would be impossible to survive and to stand before You (even for a short period). Blessed are You, Hashem, Who heals all flesh and acts wondrously.[1]

I love this prayer. It's embarrassing and perhaps a bit uncomfortably graphic, but there is a boldness and beauty in this Jewish blessing. It dares us to believe that the God who holds the planets in orbit deigns to be involved with even the most mundane, pedestrian, and scatological parts of human embodiment. It calls us to gratitude and worship in the midst of the most undignified parts of our day.

We Christians believe in a God who, by becoming human, embraced human embodiment in fullness, right down to the toenails. Because of Christ's embodiment, the ways we care for our bodies are not meaningless necessities that keep us well enough to do the real work of worship and discipleship. Instead, these small tasks of caring for our bodies, as quotidian as they are, act as an embodied confession that our Creator, who mysteriously became flesh, has made our bodies well and deserves worship in and through our very cells, muscles, tissues, and teeth.

—◆◆—

For the most part I thought seminary was a blast. I love studying doctrine and theology. I enjoy having a good theological argument (especially with friends over a meal or a drink).

But in seminary I realized that I imagined the Christian life primarily as a quest to get the right ideas in my head. I was in a brainy subculture of Christians in Cambridge, Massachusetts, which is a bit of a brainy subculture in itself—the guy who worked at the gas station by our house was often reading a philosophical tome. Being surrounded by such great minds was a gift, but I began to feel like the sort of Christianity that I gravitated toward only required my brain.

During seminary I met a family whose daughter was severely disabled. She could not speak and her brain, as far as we knew, could not sustain thought. *What would it mean for this young girl to grow in faith?* I wondered. *In what way might she worship?* I began to hunger for a faith that was not merely cognitive, not simply about achieving the right intellectual beliefs.

Being surrounded by such great minds was a gift, but I began to feel like the sort of Christianity that I gravitated toward only required my brain.

I do not want to downplay the importance of doctrine or rigorous intellectual engagement. But in the midst of theological rigor, I also yearned for ways that the Christian life worked its way into places my mind could not go.

What would it mean to believe the gospel, not just in my brain, but also in my body?

If you had asked me as a young seminarian whether Christianity valued the body, I would have most certainly said yes. I could have given you a theology of the body rooted in creation, incarnation, and resurrection, and I would have spoken about the importance of offering our bodies to God in gratitude as a "living sacrifice." Yet it wasn't enough for me to know—as simply another point of doctrine—that our bodies are important. I needed to be trained to offer my body as a living sacrifice *through my body*.

We learn how our bodies are sites of worship, not as an abstract idea, but through the practice of worshiping *with our bodies*. During seminary, I occasionally visited a little Anglican church that some friends of mine attended about forty minutes north of my house. There was a lot of movement in the service—processing, sitting, walking, standing, kneeling, eating, making the sign of the cross, reading aloud, bowing. I had been longing for an embodied faith and this church felt like some kind of spiritual Pilates class.

In his book *Earthen Vessels*, Matthew Lee Anderson argues that just as basketball players train their bodies through practice drills, "practicing the presentation of our bodies as living sacrifices in a corporate context through raising hands, lifting our eyes to the heavens, kneeling, and reciting prayers simply trains us in our whole person, body and soul, to be oriented around the throne of grace."[2]

When we eat dinner, my family sings a prayer of thanksgiving together. Before my youngest daughter could speak much, she would belt along the tune with las and ohs and inarticulate joy. She loved it. Sometimes she'd sit down and say, "Me ray! Me ray!" (Translation: "May I begin the prayer?") She didn't understand—or at least, she couldn't articulate an understanding of—what we were saying or who Jesus is or why we were singing at all. Nevertheless her body knew and was training her in a habit—a habit of pausing before she eats and singing with others in gratitude. I hope that one day she'll be able to engage her mind in rich theological study and be able to offer an articulate doctrine of prayer. Yet even now, as who she is, she can offer up a prayer with her body and join with her family in song. She is being trained in worship.

Each day our bodies are aimed toward a particular end, a telos. The way we use our bodies teaches us what our bodies are for. There are plenty of messages in our culture about this. The proliferation of pornography and sexually driven advertising trains us to understand bodies (ours and other people's) primarily as a means of conquest or pleasure. We are told that our bodies are meant to be used and abused or, on the other hand, that our bodies are meant to be worshiped.

If the church does not teach us what our bodies are for, our culture certainly will. If we don't learn to live the Christian life as embodied beings, worshiping God and stewarding the good gift of our bodies, we will learn a false gospel, an alternative liturgy of the body. Instead of temples of the Holy Spirit, we will come to see our bodies primarily as a tool for meeting our needs and desires. Or we might believe that our bodies should be flawless and spend endless amounts of time and money on creams or Botox or surgery to stave off the reality of our frail and aging bodies. Or we may attempt to ignore embodiment altogether, eating and drinking what we will, with no regard for the way our choices violate a call to steward our bodies as gifts.

If the church does not teach us what our bodies are for, our culture certainly will.

Through the practice of an embodied liturgy we learn the true telos of embodiment: Our bodies are instruments of worship.

The scandal of misusing our bodies through, for instance, sexual sin is not that God doesn't want us to enjoy our bodies or our sexuality. Instead, it is that our bodies—sacred objects intended for worship of the living God—can become a place of sacrilege.

ˋ When we use our bodies to rebel against God or to worship the false gods of sex, youth, or personal autonomy, we are not simply breaking an archaic and arbitrary commandment. We are using a sacred object—in fact, the most sacred object on earth—in a way that denigrates its beautiful and high purpose. ˈ

Sexual sin is a scandal in the Scriptures not because the apostles were blushing prigs—they were, in reality, a rather salty bunch—or because the body is dirty or evil, but because our skin and muscles and feet and hands are more sacred than any communion chalice or baptismal font. Ignoring Scripture's teaching about the proper use of the body and using our bodies for our own false worship is ↝ a misuse of the sacred akin to using consecrated bread and wine in a Wiccan goddess ceremony.

Similarly, when we denigrate our bodies—whether through neglect or staring at our faces and counting up our flaws—we are belittling a sacred site, a worship space more wondrous than the most glorious, ancient cathedral. We are standing before the Grand Canyon or the Sistine Chapel and rolling our eyes.

But when we use our bodies for their intended purpose—in gathered worship, raising our hands or singing or kneeling, or, in our average day, sleeping or savoring a meal or jumping or hiking or running or having sex with our spouse or kneeling in prayer or nursing a baby or digging a garden—it is glorious, as glorious as a great cathedral being used just as its architect had dreamt it would be.

In my tradition, when a chalice is broken or an altar cloth is torn, we don't throw it in the trash; it must be buried or burned. Leftover consecrated wine is either drunk or poured into the ground, never down the drain. We do this because these objects are sacred, set apart, and worthy of care. In the same way, care for the body—even these small, daily tasks of maintenance—is a way we honor our bodies as sacred parts of worship.

Theologian Stanley Hauerwas argues that to truly learn a story, we can't just hear it. We must also act it out. In our worship—and Hauerwas specifically cites the practices of baptism and communion—we act out the story of the gospel with and through our bodies. "We must be taught the gestures that position our bodies and our souls to be able to hear rightly and then retell the story," Hauerwas writes.

> For example, while we may be able to pray without being prostrate, I think prayer as an institution of the church could no longer be sustained without a people who have first learned to kneel. If one wants to learn to pray, one had better know how to bend the body. Learning the gesture and posture of prayer is inseparable from *learning* to pray. Indeed, the gestures are prayer.[3]

Soon after seminary I found, to my horror, that I couldn't pray. Suddenly words, which had always come so easily, fell flat. I had been through a hard year with an unwanted move, a broken relationship with a close friend, and a painful delay in my hopes for motherhood. I was hurt and grieving and could not find the words to invite God into deep places where I longed for him to meet and mend me. I felt like my words were a sad, deflated balloon tangled in branches, lifeless, stuck, and limp.

In the midst of this, though words failed me, prayer without words—prayer in and through my body—became a lifeline. I couldn't find words, but I could kneel. I could submit to God through my knees, and I'd lift my hands to hold up an ache: a fleshy, unnamable longing that I carried around my ribs. I'd offer up an aching body with my hands, my knees, my tears, my lifted eyes. My body led in prayer and led me—all of me, eventually even my words—into prayer.[4]

⬤ ◆ ⬤

One of my favorite things to do as a priest is to participate in house blessings. When people move into a new house, we come together to pray throughout their new home, moving from room to room and using a special liturgy for the occasion. My priest friend Peter has led several house blessings for people in his congregation. He told me he's noticed that everyone starts paying closer attention when they crowd into the bathroom to bless it. It may be that they are a bit uncomfortable—it's not often you crowd into a bathroom to pray with a bunch of your friends. But he's noticed that people tend to lean in and start listening more carefully, wondering what it might mean to invoke God's presence in this most humble of rooms.

He anoints the bathroom mirror with oil and prays that when people look into it, they would see themselves as beloved images of God. He prays that they would not relate to their bodies with the categories the world gives them, but instead according to the truth of who they are in Christ.

It's easy to look into the mirror and take stock of all that we feel is lacking or wrong about our bodies. Instead we must learn the habit of beholding our bodies as a gift, and learn to delight in the body God has made for us, that God loves, and that God will one day redeem and make whole. Peter told me that when he prays over the bathroom mirror, he has noticed fathers of young girls begin to cry; they long for their daughters to see themselves as God sees them, and for their reflections in their bathroom mirror to be a reflection of their belovedness and freedom in Christ.

**The bodies we use in our worship service
each week are the same bodies we take
to our kitchen table, into our bathtubs,
and under our covers at night.**

We carry all of our bodily training in gathered worship—our kneeling, singing, eating, drinking, standing, hand raising, and gesturing—with us into the bathroom on an average day when we look in the mirror. The bodies we use in our worship service each week are the same bodies we take to our kitchen table, into our bathtubs, and under our covers at night.

When I stand before the sink brushing my teeth and see my reflection in the mirror, I want it to be an act of blessing, where I remember that these teeth I'm brushing are made by God for a good purpose, that my body is inseparable from my soul, and that both deserve care. Because of the embodied work of Jesus, my body is destined for redemption and for eternal worship—for eternal skipping and jumping and twirling and hand raising and kneeling and dancing and singing and chewing and tasting.

This is a great mystery. My teeth will be in eternity and are eternally good.

When I brush my teeth I am pushing back, in the smallest of ways, the death and chaos that will inevitably overtake my body. I am dust polishing dust. And yet I am not only dust. When God formed people from the dust, he breathed into us—through our lips and teeth—his very breath.

So I will fight against my body's fallenness. I will care for it as best I can, knowing that my body is sacred and that caring for it (and for the other bodies around me) is a holy act. I'll hold on to the truth that my body, in all its brokenness, is beloved, and that one day it will be, like the resurrected body of Christ, glorious. Brushing my teeth, therefore, is a nonverbal prayer, an act of worship that claims the hope to come. My minty breath—a little foretaste of glory.

4

losing keys

confession and the truth about ourselves

I have a plan for my morning—run by the store to pick up a side for dinner and some dish soap, then head to a meeting.

So after I brush my teeth and help Jonathan get the kids off to their activities, I get dressed quickly and eat breakfast. I throw on my favorite corduroy coat, hoist my computer bag over my shoulder, and head toward the door. I go to grab the car keys on the entry table that we bought (and painted robin's egg blue) for the express purpose of having a spot for keys. Next to the jar of dried lavender and stack of mail are two key rings that hold the keys to the car, the house, and our neighbor's house, as well as a couple others the purpose of which I've forgotten (but I keep holding on to them because you never know).

Cue the sound of screeching brakes. The keys aren't there.

I check the side pocket of my bag, then the pants I wore yesterday, then my bag again. I start to panic a little. I take off my coat. I walk into my kitchen and look on the counter.

I have lost my keys. With them goes all sense of perspective. With them goes my plan; with them goes my cool. These instruments that I use for security and freedom—to lock out bad guys and get where I need to go—have suddenly become a means of imprisonment. I'm stuck.

Where could they be?

I go through my Stages of Searching for Lost Objects:

Stage 1. *Logic.* I retrace my steps. I look in the places that make sense. I breathe. I try to remain calm and rational: This is not that big of a deal. They'll turn up.

Stage 2. *Self-condemnation.* As I make my way through each room, scanning shelves and surfaces, I begin to self-flagellate under my breath: "I am such an idiot. Where did I put those keys? Why am I such an idiot?"

Stage 3. *Vexation.* I get frustrated. I curse. Each second that passes leaves me slightly angrier. I switch back and forth between blaming myself and blaming others. My kids. They probably played with them and lost them. Did Jonathan take them? I text him. No help there. God must know where my keys are. Why isn't he helping here? I'm having a mild theological crisis over a two-inch piece of metal.

Stage 4. *Desperation.* I start looking everywhere, even places that don't make sense. I'm rummaging through random drawers and looking under beds, checking the pants pocket that I've already checked three times, grumbling.

I check the time. It's been nine minutes.

Stage 5. *Last-ditch.* I stop and pray. Okay, breathe. I tell myself that I'm being ridiculous, that I'm overreacting. Calm down. I quickly ask God for a restoration of perspective. I remember that a Catholic friend once told me to ask Saint Anthony to pray for us when we've lost something. So, for good measure, I murmur as I check my sock drawer, "Uh, Saint Anthony, not sure how this works, but if you can hear me, can you please pray for me to find my keys?"

Stage 6. *Despair*. I give up and plop on the couch. I will never find my keys. The cause is hopeless. I am hopeless. I will be trapped here until the end of time or until we shell out the money to replace them. Outside the window, by my locked car, are naked trees and hopping sparrows, but I will not notice. Everything is worthless. The morning is ruined. Stupid keys. Stupid me. Stupid planet. Stupid universe.

Then, a bit ashamed and guilty about my overreaction, I pull myself together and, beginning at step one, repeat the cycle.

Seven minutes later, I find my keys under the couch. I have no idea how they got there. I yelp to no one in particular, "Found them!" Cue the Hallelujah chorus.

I will quickly move on. Out the driveway. Skip the grocery store and head straight to the meeting. My lost keys ended up being a hiccup in the day, no big deal, a tiny, forgettable fifteen minutes.

But it was also the apocalypse.

Apocalypse literally means an unveiling or uncovering. In my anger, grumbling, self-berating, cursing, doubt, and despair, I glimpsed, for a few minutes, how tightly I cling to control and how little control I actually have. And in the absence of control, feeling stuck and stressed, those parts of me that I prefer to keep hidden were momentarily unveiled.

◆◆◆

Sometimes my days run smoothly. Like ticker tape, they hum along, pleasant enough, productive at times—my plans, for the most part, uninterrupted. And then something small happens, the slightest tear in the tape, and the whole thing halts and becomes an unbidden morality tale. The neediness and sinfulness, neurosis and weakness that I try to pretty up and manage through control, ease, and privilege are suddenly on display.

A few weeks ago the dryer, the dishwasher, and the ceiling fan all broke within a few hours. Most of my adult life I have had neither a dryer (we used a clothesline or the laundromat), nor a dishwasher (we did the dishes by hand), nor ceiling fans (we have air conditioning), but when they all broke simultaneously it felt like the universe had me on some kind of hit list. I took it personally.

Small things go wrong. I feel hurried or overwhelmed, burdened by sad news or worried for a friend, and like a rising flood, inch by inch, the collective sadness and frustration mounts and I snap. I yell at my daughters to quiet down. I slam the broken dishwasher door just a bit harder than necessary. I mutter something under my breath. If I were a lioness, I would snarl. As it is, I brood.

These unbidden unveilings in my day are insignificant compared to the immense suffering in our lives and in the broader world. There are people who face profound agony every day: chronic pain, heart-wrenching loss, desperation. In my own life there have been seasons of deep sorrow. But this is not that. This is not the Valley of the Shadow of Death. This is the roadside ditch of broken things and lost objects, the potholes of gloom and unwanted interruptions.

And yet here is where I find myself on an ordinary day, and here, in my petty anger and irritation, is where the Savior deigns to meet me.

These moments are an opportunity for formation, for sanctification. Underneath these overreactions and aggravations lie true fears. My lost keys reveal my anxiety that I won't be able to do what I need to do to take care of myself and those around me. They hit on my fear of failure and incompetency. My broken dishwasher uncovers my worries about money—will we have enough to fix it? And it exposes my idolatry of ease, my false hope in comfort and convenience—I just want things to run smoothly.

Today my lost keys provide a moment of revelation, revealing the lostness inside me and my misplaced reliance.

When the day is lovely and sunny and everything is going according to plan, I can look like a pretty good person. But little things gone wrong and interrupted plans reveal who I really am; my cracks show and I see that I am profoundly in need of grace.

But here's the thing: pretty good people do not need Jesus. He came for the lost. He came for the broken. In his love for us he came to usher us into his foundness and wholeness.

◆ ◆ ◆

Paul tells us to be content in all circumstances (Phil 4:11). For Paul that meant finding contentment amid shipwrecks, beatings, and persecution. But I need not wait around for a shipwreck to prove my contentment in all circumstances. The call to contentment is a call amidst the concrete circumstances I find myself in today. I need to find joy and reject despair in the moment I'm in, in the midst of small pressures and needling anxieties.

There is a theological term, *theodicy*, that names the painful mystery of how God can be powerful and good and still allow bad things to happen. Discussions of theodicy rightly tend to be about large-scale horrors: How can God allow war, famine, and the suffering of children?

When suffering is sharp and profound, I expect and believe that God will meet me in its midst. But in the struggles of my average day I somehow feel I have a right to be annoyed. The indignations and irritations of the modern world feel authentic and understandable. I'm no Pollyanna. In a shipwreck, yes of course, "Be content." But the third day in a row of poor sleep and a backed-up sink? That's too much to ask. In *Letters to Malcolm*, C. S. Lewis says that people are "merely 'amusing themselves' by asking for patience which a famine or a persecution would call for if, in the meantime, the weather and every other inconvenience sets them grumbling."[1]

The call to contentment is a call amidst the concrete circumstances I find myself in today.

I spent a few months in a war-torn area of the world and was surprised to find that there, in the midst of tensions and dangers, I felt far more at peace than in my average American, housebound day with a baby and a toddler. I had a theology of suffering that allowed me to pay attention in crisis, to seek small flickers of mercy in profound darkness. But my theology was too big to touch a typical day in my life. I'd developed the habit of ignoring God in the midst of the daily grind.

Rod Dreher writes about his struggle with despair in an average day. "Everydayness is my problem. It's easy to think about what you would do in wartime, or if a hurricane blows through, or if you spent a month in Paris, or if your guy wins the election, or if you won the lottery or bought that thing you really wanted. It's a lot more difficult to figure out how you're going to get through today without despair."[2]

I can't simply will myself to, as Paul says, "do all things without grumbling or disputing" (Phil 2:14). It's not enough to merely want to be more content or to tell myself to cheer up. I need to cultivate the practice of meeting Christ in these small moments of grief, frustration, and anger, of encountering Christ's death and resurrection—this big story of brokenness and redemption—in a small, gray, stir-crazy Tuesday morning.

Otherwise, I'll spend my life imagining and hoping (and preaching and teaching about how) to share in the sufferings of Christ in persecution, momentous suffering, and death, while I spend my actual days in grumbling, discontentment, and low-grade despair.

—◆—◆—◆—

For some of us, the idea of repentance can bring to mind a particular emotional experience, or the minor-key songs of an altar call at a revival meeting. But repentance and faith are the constant, daily rhythms of the Christian life, our breathing out and breathing in.

In these small moments that reveal my lostness and brokenness, I need to develop the habit of admitting the truth of who I am—not running to justify myself or minimize my sin. And yet, in my brokenness and lostness, I also need to form the habit of letting God love me, trusting again in his mercy, and receiving again his words of forgiveness and absolution over me. Rich Mullins, one of my favorite writers and musicians, said that when he was a kid he'd walk down the church aisle and be "born again again" or "rededicate" his life to Christ every year at camp. In college he'd do it about every six months, then quarterly; by the time he was in his forties it was "about four times a day."[3] Repentance is not usually a moment wrought in high drama. It is the steady drumbeat of a life in Christ and, therefore, a day in Christ.

In church each week, we repent together. We confess that we have sinned "in thought, word, and deed, by what we have done, and by what we have left undone," that we have neglected to love God with our whole hearts, and our neighbors as ourselves.[4] This practice of communal confession is a vital way to enact the habit of confession that marks our daily lives. Through it we learn together the language of repentance and faith.

Confession reminds us that none of us gather for worship because we are "pretty good people." But we are new people, people marked by grace in spite of ourselves because of the work of Christ. Our communal practice of confession reminds us that failure in the Christian life is the norm. We—each and all—take part in gathered worship as unworthy people who, left on our own, deserve God's condemnation. But we are not left on our own.

Repentance is not usually a moment wrought in high drama. It is the steady drumbeat of a life in Christ and, therefore, a day in Christ.

Our failures or successes in the Christian life are not what define us or determine our worth before God or God's people. Instead, we are defined by Christ's life and work on our behalf. We kneel. We humble ourselves together. We admit the truth. We confess and repent. Together, we practice the posture that we embrace each day— that of a broken and needy people who receive abundant mercy.

And then—what a wonder!—the word of absolution: "Almighty God have mercy on you, forgive you all your sins through our Lord Jesus Christ, strengthen you in all goodness, and by the power of the Holy Spirit keep you in eternal life."[5] In Anglican liturgical practice we never confess without also hearing God's blessing and forgiveness over us. In traditional liturgical churches the priest stands and pronounces absolution. The priest asks God for mercy and forgiveness through Jesus' work on our behalf.

Once a close friend visited my church, and she was concerned by this part of our service. She didn't like that the priest pronounced absolution. She asked, "Don't we receive forgiveness from God, not a priest?" Why use a go-between? I told her that forgiveness is from God, and yet I still need to be told. I need to hear in a loud voice that I am forgiven and loved, a voice that is truer, louder, and more tangible than the accusing voices within and without that tell me I'm not.

When we confess and receive absolution together, we are reminded that none of our pathologies, neuroses, or sins, no matter how small or secret, affect only us. We are a church, a community, a family. We are not simply individuals with our pet sins and private brokenness. We are people who desperately need each other if we are to seek Christ and walk in repentance. If we are saved, we are saved together—as the body of Christ, as a church. Because of this, I need to hear my forgiveness proclaimed not only by God but by a representative of the body of Christ in which I receive grace, to remind me that though my sin is worse than I care to admit, I'm still welcome here. I'm still called into this community and loved.

Unkind and condemning thoughts tell me that God's love is distant, cold or irrelevant, that I must prove myself to God and other people, that I am orphaned and unlovable, that God is tapping his toe, impatient with me, ready to walk out on me. These thoughts are loud enough that I need a human voice telling me, week in and week out, that they're lies. I need to hear from someone who knows me that there is grace enough for me, that Christ's work is on my behalf, even as I'm on my knees confessing that I've blown it again this week. We may confess quietly, even silently. But we are reminded of our forgiveness out loud, with standing and shouting. We need to be sure to hear it.

------ ◆ ◆ ◆ ------

In these moments of my day—losing keys, losing patience, snapping at those I love, slamming the dishwasher door—I can respond with self-condemnation, self-justification, or repentance. When we confess and receive absolution together, we are like a football team practicing its plays, or a theater company rehearsing its lines. Together as a church we are practicing, learning the strokes that teach us to live our lives.

The practice of confession and absolution must find its way into the small moments of sinfulness in my day. When it does, the gospel—grace itself—seeps into my day, and these moments are transformed. They're no longer meaningless interruptions, sheer failure and lostness and brokenness. Instead, they're moments of redemption and remembering, moments to grow bit by bit in trusting Jesus' work on my behalf.

Over time, through the daily practices of confession and absolution, I learn to look for God in the cracks of my day, to notice what these moments of failure reveal about who I am—my false hopes and false gods. I learn to invite the true God into the reality of my lostness and brokenness, to agree with him about my sin and to hear again his words of blessing, acceptance, and love.

When Jesus was approached by some "pretty good people" who were offended that he hung out with sinners, he compared God to a woman who had lost something. God's eager love for us ventures into the undignified and outsized, like a woman who is a little over the top about a lost coin, sweeping out rooms and looking under the furniture until she finds it. God searches more earnestly for me than I do for my keys. He is zealous to find his people and to make them whole.

5

eating leftovers

Word, sacrament, and overlooked nourishment

I grew up eating processed food. Each morning I'd have Eggo waffles with my dad. After school, if I was lucky, my Mom would give me bright pink Quik strawberry milk. My very favorite food was Kraft Mac and Cheese.

I have blissful childhood memories of helping harvest corn at my grandparents' house and feasting on sweet, buttery piles of it for dinner, but besides that I never really thought about where my food came from. I never considered my meal's environmental impact, the working conditions of those who harvested my tomatoes, or why the milk was pink.

Soon after we were married, Jonathan and I discovered the writing of Michael Pollan and Wendell Berry, both of whom critique the industrial food system and extol the virtues of eating food that is local, homegrown, and organic. We began, very slowly, to change the way we ate. We started going to farmers' markets, joined a community-supported agriculture co-op, and have attempted (mostly, but not entirely, unsuccessfully) to grow a vegetable garden.

I've always loved food. I like to make it, to eat it, and to read and talk about it. And now I have some soaring ideals about it.

I love food, in part, because it is necessary for life and for the care of my body and the bodies of those I love (and feed). But I also love food for metaphorical reasons. Food has so much to teach us about nourishment, and as a culture we struggle with what it means to be not simply fed, but profoundly and holistically nourished. It is a joy to sit at the table with nourishing food and be able to tell stories—nourishing stories—about where each dish came from: the Amish woman who sold me the squash, or the unlikely survival of an eggplant in our otherwise-failed garden.

In my mind I have an ideal for my table—friends and family gathered around a homegrown, local, organic feast with candles and laughter and well-behaved children. A lot of beauty and a lot of butter.

But much of the time, my meals aren't like that.

And today, I have leftovers for lunch.

Taco soup. Not homegrown. Not local. Corn and beans dumped from cans into a crockpot. It's a go-to meal for us, what we make when people are coming over because it is cheap and easy. It is adequate and a little boring. Now, it is warmed over again on my stove for lunch.

Like most of what I'll eat in this life, it's necessary and forgettable.

❖ ❖ ❖

Christian worship is arranged around two things: Word and sacrament.

The Word, in this context, refers to the Scriptures, both read and preached. The sacraments, for most Protestants, are baptism and Communion, also called the Eucharist.[1] Together, Word and sacrament are, inseparably, the centerpieces of Christian worship. The reading and preaching of Scripture is fulfilled and completed by the proclamation of the gospel in the Communion meal. Communion, in turn, is interpreted and given context by the preaching of the Word.

And both Word and sacrament are profoundly related to food. These two central acts of worship, Scripture and Communion, are compared to my bowl of taco soup, my daily bread. Both are necessary because both, together, are our nourishment.

In Ezekiel and again in Revelation we find the startling image of God commanding his prophets to eat the scroll—the words of God set before them (Ezek 3:1-3; Rev 10:9-10). In his temptation in the wilderness Christ says that we are not only nourished by bread but by "every word that comes from the mouth of God" (Mt 4:4). Later, Paul compares God's teachings to milk and solid food (1 Cor 3:2).

At the Last Supper Jesus tells his disciples to eat in remembrance of him. Of all the things he could've chosen to be done "in remembrance" of him, Jesus chose a meal. He could have asked his followers to do something impressive or mystical—climb a mountain, fast for forty days, or have a trippy sweat lodge ceremony—but instead he picks the most ordinary of acts, eating, through which to be present to his people. He says that the bread is his body and the wine is his blood. He chooses the unremarkable and plain, average and abundant, bread and wine.

N. T. Wright reminds us that in the upper room, right before Jesus' death, he didn't offer his followers theories of the atonement

63

or recite a creed or explain precisely how his death would accomplish salvation. Instead "he gave them an act to perform. Specifically, he gave them a meal to share. It is a meal that speaks more volumes than any theory."[2]

If all the cathedrals on earth were gone, all the most glorious art were lost, and all of the world's most valuable treasures were thrown out, Christians could and would still meet for worship around the Scriptures and the Eucharist. To have church, all we need is Word and sacrament.

And both Word and sacrament are gifts given by Jesus, who calls himself the bread of life. The Word of God and the meal of God's people are intended to point to and make manifest the presence of Christ, who is both the Word and the bread. In John 6, Jesus reminds his listeners that they received manna, their daily bread, as a gift from the Father, but that it was not enough to nourish them spiritually. They still died. But Jesus promises that those who eat "bread from heaven" will be eternally nourished and will not die. Then, to the horror of his disciples, he says that this heavenly bread is his very flesh and calls them to feed on it as their "true food" (Jn 6:55).

Christ is our bread and gives us bread. He is the gift and the giver. God gives us every meal we eat, and every meal we eat is ultimately partial and inadequate, pointing to him who is our true food, our eternal nourishment.

◆ ◆ ◆

I briefly bow my head and thank God for my taco soup, a daily ritual so ingrained in me that I pause in gratitude before this meal without much thought. But this habit of prayer reminds me to receive the day and all it contains as a gift. In his book *Food and Faith*, Norman Wirzba tells us that "to say grace before a meal is among the highest and most honest expressions of our humanity.... Here, around the table and before witnesses, we testify to the experience of life as a precious gift to be received and given again. We acknowledge that we do not and cannot live alone but are the beneficiaries of the kindness and mysteries of grace upon grace."[3]

In college I became friends with a chain-smoking Franciscan monk. One day I was telling him about a gift someone had given me—a gift that felt too extravagant to receive. I asked him if I should refuse, if it was wrong to accept such an unneeded luxury. As a Franciscan friar, I figured he would encourage me toward simplicity and against extravagance. Instead, he quoted Luke 10 (and the Franciscan rule), and told me that Saint Francis would say, "Eat such things as are set before you."[4] He told me that I needed to learn to receive from God and others, in trust and gratitude.

This moment of pause before my meal conditions me to learn to eat such things as are set before me, to receive the nourishment available in this day as a gift, whether it looks like extravagant abundance, painful suffering, or simply a boring bowl of leftovers.

◆ ◆ ◆

There are a few very goods meals I remember and there are a few truly terrible meals I remember. But most of the meals I've eaten, thousands upon thousands, were utterly unremarkable. If you asked me what I ate for lunch three weeks ago on Monday, I could not tell you. And yet that average, forgettable meal nourished me. Thousands of forgotten meals have brought me to today. They've sustained my life. They were my daily bread.

We are endlessly in need of nourishment, and nourishment comes, usually, like taco soup. Abundant and overlooked.

My subculture of evangelicalism tends to focus on excitement, passion, and risk, the kind of worship that gives a rush. Eugene Peterson calls this quest for spiritual intensity a consumer-driven "market for religious experience in our world." He says that "there is little enthusiasm for the patient acquisition of virtue, little inclination to sign up for a long apprenticeship in what earlier generations of Christians called holiness. Religion in our time has been captured by a tourist mindset. . . . We go to see a new personality, to hear a new truth, to get a new experience and so somehow to expand our otherwise humdrum life."[5]

We contemporary evangelicals come by this honestly. We've inherited a faith that, while beautiful in many ways, was formed and shaped by the concept of a market-driven religious experience. Historian Harry Stout writes that in George Whitefield, one of America's first evangelical preachers, "Charity, preaching, and journalism came together . . . to create a potent configuration—a religious celebrity capable of creating a new market for religion."[6] In this market-driven faith, intense or ecstatic religious experience was emphasized and even sometimes contrived. Lorenzo Dow, an early American evangelist, would smash chairs or arrange for a trumpet to blow at key moments during his preaching. Charles Finney's preaching was "punctuated by moments of high drama such as his vivid evocation of the smoke of the torment of sinners in hell, prompting his audience to imagine that they could see it themselves."[7]

Instead of the focus of worship being that which nourishes us, namely Word and sacrament, the focus became that which sells:

excitement, adventure, a sizzling or shocking spiritual experience. An individual's own experience of worship, a subjective notion of his or her encounter with God, became the centerpiece of the Christian life.

There are indeed moments of spiritual ecstasy in the Christian life and in gathered worship. Powerful spiritual experiences, when they come, are a gift. But that cannot be the point of Christian spirituality, any more than the unforgettable pappardelle pasta dish I ate years ago in Boston's North End is the point of eating.

Word and sacrament sustain my life, and yet they often do not seem life changing. Quietly, even forgettably, they feed me.

There are times when we approach Scripture, whether in private study or gathered worship, and find it powerful and memorable— sermons we quote and carry around with us, stories we tell of being impacted and changed. There are other times when the Scriptures seem as unappetizing as stale bread. I'm bored or confused or skeptical or repulsed. There are times when I walk away from Scripture with more questions than answers.

We can be like the dwarves in C. S. Lewis's Narnian tales who have a delectable feast set before them but, because of a curse, mistake it for food that is revolting, unappetizing, perhaps even poisonous.[8]

How should we respond when we find the Word perplexing or dry or boring or unappealing?

We keep eating. We receive nourishment. We keep listening and learning and taking our daily bread. We wait on God to give us what we need to sustain us one more day. We acknowledge that there is far more wonder in this life of worship than we yet have eyes to see or stomachs to digest. We receive what has been set before us today as a gift.

◆ ◆ ◆

In these leftovers, I'm surrounded by almost unimaginable abundance. Here, on my table, is a steaming symbol of my astounding privilege—so much taco soup that we could not eat it all and were able to keep it for days because, through a process I can't even comprehend, humans discovered electricity and found that compressed tetrafluoroethane gas running through coils can keep food at just the right temperature for its maximal preservation.

This abundance, the sheer amount and variety of food and the ability to keep it for days, would astound much of the world and most people throughout history. But I have been dulled to the wonders before me. I take this nourishment for granted.

This habit of praying before my meal trains me in a way of being-in-the-world. It reminds me that my personal experience is not what determines whether or not something is a grace and a wonder, and that some of the most astonishing gifts are the most easily overlooked.

◆ ◆ ◆

These forgotten meals shape and form me. Anyone who has ever changed their diet—cut out gluten or become a vegetarian or begun eating healthier—can tell you that habits shape us, meal by meal. In the same way, I am shaped almost imperceptibly by Word and sacrament. They develop in me, over time, a palate for truth. At its best, gathered worship forms me not as a spiritual-experience consumer but as a person who is, as the *Book of Common Prayer* puts it, "fed with spiritual food."[9]

In college, I liked ramen noodles. The main reason I liked them, besides the fact that they were awesomely terrible and cheap, was because we didn't have a kitchen in our dorm room. All our meals had to come from "The Pit," the charming nickname for our cafeteria. But my suitemate, Jen, had a camp stove and we had a sink so, by the magic of Maruchan ramen, we could make lunch in our dorm room. We got into the routine of doing this together almost daily, sitting on Jen's futon, eating our instant ramen. There was hardly any nourishment in it, besides the good conversation with Jen, but it left us feeling full enough and we didn't have to slog across campus. Plus, once you start eating ramen, it's hard to stop. It's addictive.

Habits shape our desires. I desired ramen noodles more than good, nourishing food because, over time, I had taught myself to crave certain things and not others. In the same way I am either formed by the practices of the church into a worshiper who can receive all of life as a gift, or I am formed, inevitably, as a mere consumer, even a consumer of spirituality. The contemporary church can, at times, market a kind of "ramen noodle" spirituality. Faith becomes a consumer product—it asks little of us, affirms our values, and promises to meet our needs, but in the end it's just a quick fix that leaves us glutted and malnourished.

❖ ❖ ❖

There is a whole industry that would like me to believe that this taco soup is just soup, merely a commodity, a product to be consumed, with nothing at all to say about morality or what it means to be human. Eating this way causes me to forget where my food comes from, to ignore its connection to the land and to the people who grew and harvested it. The sacrifices this soup represents— from both people and animals—are invisible to me.

If I were eating this soup a century ago, it would likely have come to me through land I had tilled or through a farmer I knew and could talk to and live life with. This kind of embedded community and commerce links us to those who we owe gratitude—our neighbors, our land, and ultimately, God.

But now this taco soup is an anonymous commodity. It arrives on my table seemingly by magic. With this anonymity comes ingratitude—I do not recall those farmers and harvesters to whom I owe a debt of thanks. I do not think of God's mercy in providing a harvest.

And with anonymity and ingratitude comes injustice. Like so much of what we consume in our complicated world of global capitalism and multinational corporations, purchasing this corn and these beans involves me, however unwittingly, in webs of systemic injustice, exploitation, and environmental degradation that I am ignorant about and would likely not consent to. I do not know where the onions in my soup came from or how the workers who harvested them were treated. My leftovers may have been provided by a man whose kids can't afford lunch today.[10]

Despite what a culture of consumerism may lead me to believe, my leftovers are not theologically neutral. This soup is a product of our "global theology." Ira Jackson has said, "We have a global theology without morality, without a Bible. It only offers a transaction manual for wealth creation and the efficient allocation of capital."[11] The corporations that sold me the beans, corn, and onions in this soup name me only as a consumer. Our relationship is solely transactional—I need certain goods and services to live, and they provide them for a profit.

Christian worship, centered on Word and sacrament, reminds me that my core identity is not that of a consumer: I am a worshiper and an image-bearer, created to know, enjoy, and glorify God and to know and love those around me. These anonymous kidney beans say that what mainly matters about me is the fact that I need to buy things to stay alive. But God knows the harvester of these beans and cares about justice. And God has made us not merely to consume but to cultivate, steward, and bless.

The word *Eucharist* literally means "thanksgiving." The Eucharist is the thanksgiving feast of the church, and it is out of that communal practice of thanksgiving that my lunchtime prayer of thanks flows. The Eucharist—our gathered meal of thanksgiving for the life, death, and resurrection of Christ—transforms each humble meal into a moment to recall that we receive all of life, from soup to salvation, by grace. As such, these small, daily moments are sacramental—not that they are sacraments themselves, but that God meets us in and through the earthy, material world in which we dwell.

The Eucharist is a profoundly communal meal that reorients us from people who are merely individualistic consumers into people who are, together, capable of imaging Christ in the world. Of course, eating itself reminds us that none of us can stay alive on our own. If you are breathing, it's because someone fed you. We are born hungry and completely dependent on others to meet our needs. In this way the act of eating reorients us from an atomistic, independent existence toward one that is interdependent. But the Eucharist goes even further. In it, we feast on Christ, and are thereby mysteriously formed together into one body, the body of Christ.

Nourishment is always far more than biological nutrition. We are nourished by our communities. We are nourished by gratitude. We are nourished by justice. We are nourished when we know and love our neighbors.

When we see food as a mere commodity and ourselves as mere consumers, holistic nourishment is a secondary concern. Our primary concern is that our meal is convenient, cheap, plentiful, and requires very little from us. The habits that led me to make this soup were not borne of my formation as a steward and a worshiper but of my formation as a consumer.

The free-market economy can produce a kind of abundance. I have more than enough soup. And yet this appearance of abundance is false when it comes at the cost of subjecting others to slave labor or poisoning the soil.

The habits that led me to make this soup were not borne of my formation as a steward and a worshiper but of my formation as a consumer.

This "global theology" of consumerism has transformed both the way we eat and the way we worship. The evangelical quest for a particular emotional experience in worship and the capitalistic quest for anonymous, cheap canned goods have something in common. Both are mostly concerned with what I can get for myself as an individual consumer.

But the economy of the Eucharist calls me to a life of self-emptying worship.

We must guard against those practices—both in the church and in our daily life—that shape us into mere consumers. Spirituality packaged as a path to personal self-fulfillment and happiness fits neatly into Western consumerism. But the Scriptures and the sacraments reorient us to be people who feed on the bread of life together and are sent out as stewards of redemption. We recall and reenact Christ's life poured out for us, and we are transformed into people who pour out our lives for others.[12]

We are formed by our habits of consumption.

And in contemporary America, this daily formation is often at odds with our formation in Word and sacrament. In this alternative economy of the true bread of life, we are turned inside out so that we are no longer people marked by scarcity, jockeying for our own good, but are new people, truly nourished, and therefore able to extend nourishment to others. The economy of the Eucharist is true abundance. There is enough for me, not in spite of others, but because we receive Christ together as a community.

Word and sacrament—Scripture and Eucharist—transform my midweek leftovers. They transform me from a mindless consumer into someone capable of Eucharistic interdependence and gratitude. They teach me to receive these leftovers—and all of life—as a gift.

And yet they also serve as a judgment on my meal, a call to repentance for the systems of scarcity and injustice that I perpetuate in my average day. They call me to work toward a new way of being—and eating—that allows me to better know, love, and serve my neighbors. They challenge me to empty myself for others, knowing that I will be filled to the brim over and over again in the abundant economy of worship. In Christ there will always be enough for us, with so much left over.

6

fighting
with my husband

**passing the peace and the everyday
work of shalom**

Jonathan stopped by at midday to pick something up at the house, and we had a fight. I would call it an argument, but that sounds too reasonable, like we were coolly debating opposing sides of an issue. Logical. Rational. Collected. The stuff to make marriage therapists proud.

This was hardly that.

Because most often what we're arguing about—in this case a decision about our daughter's schooling—isn't really what we're arguing about. What we are actually arguing about is our fears, anxieties, identities, and hopes. We were really arguing about how we love our daughter and feel a chasm—a terrifying chasm—between our responsibility for her and our ability to bear it well.

74

We were grieving the reality of our limitedness and our inability to rescue our daughter from suffering in our broken world—and even in our broken family.

And we were arguing about the sharpness in our voices, and who interrupts whom, and how often, and about a passing comment he made yesterday and a look I gave this morning.

These are the patterns in family life that make it hard to be patient and gentle and kind. I'm not mad that you threw your shirt on the floor today; I'm mad about the last three hundred times you've thrown your shirt on the floor. Or, more painfully, it's not just that I'm mad about your criticism today, it's how a pattern of criticism, comment by passing comment, bumps up against my own patterns of sin, woundedness, and self-defensiveness.

Today's conflict is not a marital crisis—there was no profound betrayal or lie or scandal. It is a bur-under-the-saddle conflict over the kind of habitual resentment that, if we let it, builds. We start by talking about something casual. Then I fret aloud and he dismisses it—because I've fretted aloud so often that it is a pattern—and I say something sarcastic and it escalates from there until one or both of us yells and then one or both of us leaves the room.

Thankfully, we have a small house—we can't get too far away from each other. So we play chicken. I sigh loudly. He gets on the computer. We wait to see who will lay down their sword first. It takes a lot of bravery to lay down a sword—more bravery than either of us have at the moment. So we sit in stony silence.

◆ ◆ ◆

The truth is I get along with most people pretty well. When I do have conflict, it is usually with those I love most. The struggle to "love thy neighbor" is most often tested in my home, with my husband and my kids, when I'm tired, fearful, discouraged, off my game, or just want to be left alone.

I'm a pacifist who yells at her husband.

For most of my twenties, I was part of a movement in evangelicalism that valued a radical, edgy kind of faith—I wanted to change the world, at least a little part of it. I wanted to be part of a community that sought justice and that served "the least of these." What drew me to that kind of work, besides the clear call of Scripture, was a longing for and vision of God's shalom—a very pregnant word that means God's all-consuming, all-redeeming peace. The hope of a kingdom where God is worshiped wholly, where humanity extends love and mercy with generosity, where systemic injustice is broken and "the oppressed are set free" was (and is) inconceivably beautiful and intoxicating. So I worked among the homeless, lived briefly in a couple of Christian communities, and worked in churches trying to connect upper middle-class folks with those in poverty. I fell in love with the writings of Dorothy Day and Saint Francis and I wanted to go overseas to work among "the poorest of the poor."

Now that I'm a bit older and a wife and mom, the radiant vision of God's kingdom remains immensely compelling to me. And yet, though I profess big ideas about the beauty of shalom and Christ's ministry of peace crashing into our world, I often find myself squabbling and quarrelling my way through the day—with those I love the most. I'm a pacifist who yells at her husband.

The band Waterdeep has a song that begins, "You talk of hating war. But where's your own peacetime?"[1] I can get caught up in big ideas of justice and truth and neglect the small opportunities around me to extend kindness, forgiveness, and grace.

In C. S. Lewis's *Screwtape Letters*, senior demon Screwtape coaches a junior devil on how to infect a man's relationship with others: "Keep his mind off the most elementary of duties by directing it to the most advanced and spiritual ones. Aggravate that most useful of human characteristics, the horror and neglect of the obvious."[2] He continues, "I have had patients of my own so well in hand that they could be turned at a moment's notice from impassioned prayer for a wife's or son's 'soul' to beating or insulting the real wife or son without a qualm."[3]

Like those under Screwtape's influence, I often neglect the obvious, proclaiming a radical love for the world even as I neglect to care for those closest to me.

But I am increasingly aware that I cannot seek God's peace and mission in the world without beginning right where I am, in my home, in my neighborhood, in my church, with the real people right around me.

〰 ◆ ◆ ◆ 〰

At church on Sunday morning, right before the Eucharist, we pass the peace. At the churches I've been to, this mostly looks like chaos. Parishioners turn to each other and say "Peace of Christ to you" or "Peace of the Lord" or "Hey" or "My name is Jim." Kids run around the sanctuary. People talk. It's loud. Congregants walk to and fro, in and out of the sanctuary. The gregarious mingle and laugh. Others shift awkwardly, not quite sure what to do, waiting to just get on with it.

The passing of the peace falls right between the sermon and the Eucharist, smack dab between Word and sacrament. After we've heard the Holy Scriptures preached and before a profoundly mysterious, sacred meal, we stop and let everyone run wild for a few minutes.

The timing isn't an oversight or poor liturgical planning. It isn't included to give folks a chance to stretch their legs or take a bathroom break. The passing of peace is placed where it is in the liturgy for theological reasons. Before we come to the Eucharist, before we take the body and blood of Christ, we actively extend peace to the members of the body of Christ right around us. It's a liturgical enactment of the reality that we cannot approach the table of the Prince of Peace if we aren't at peace with our neighbor.

This practice of passing the peace has been part of Christian worship since the dawn of the church—and our early Christian brothers and sisters didn't settle for a handshake or awkward side-hug; they kissed each other—a practice which emerged in part from the ancient Jewish custom of greeting guests with a kiss before a meal.[4] Early Christians were so intent on ensuring that the passing of the peace was a time of real reconciliation and not a mere formality that in third-century Eastern churches a deacon would stand up during the passing of the peace and cry, "Is there any man that keepeth aught against his fellow?"[5] Early Christians took seriously Jesus' teaching in Matthew 5 that if someone is approaching the altar and remembers that their brother has something against them, they must leave and go make peace with the offended brother before offering a gift to God.

So before the meal of peace, we speak peace to those nearest us. More than once, Jonathan and I have had to get up in the middle of the passing of the peace and go outside to talk through an argument we had on the way to church.

A friend of mine, a Presbyterian pastor, once remarked to me that each week when my four-year-old passes the peace, she is being formed in a particular worldview. She is practicing the truth that the extension of peace is vital to worship, that worshiping God is inextricably tied with seeking God's kingdom of shalom by making peace with her neighbors. Through her church community, my daughter is being trained as a peacemaker.

When we pass the peace we are acting out how we live as believers in mission each day. Dom Gregory Dix, a twentieth-century Anglican monk and priest, wrote that the passing of the peace is the "solemn putting into act before God of the whole Christian living of the church's members."[6]

The passing of the peace finds its way into our day mostly in small, unseen moments as we live together, seeking to love those people who are the constants, the furniture in our lives—parents, spouses, kids, friends, enemies, the barista we chat with each week as we wait for coffee, the people in the pew behind us with the noisy toddler, the old man next door who doesn't get out much.

In these tiny, unseen interactions we reenact the passing of the peace that we practice on Sunday. "Peace of Christ to you" is instantiated as I hand my toddler carrot sticks, respond patiently to Jonathan when I feel slighted, or genuinely celebrate a friend's upcoming vacation even though I'd never be able to afford it myself. Ordinary love, anonymous and unnoticed as it is, is the substance of peace on earth, the currency of God's grace in our daily life.

We can sometimes separate the big idea of shalom-seeking from the ordinary warp and woof of life. We make false dichotomies between private and public, between social justice and "family values." But in Christian worship we are reminded that peace is homegrown, beginning on the smallest scale, in the daily grind, in homes, churches, and neighborhoods. Daily habits of peace or habits of discord spill into our city, creating cultures of peace or cultures of discord.

———◆◆◆———

The prophet Jeremiah reminds us that the peace of our small sphere and the broader peace of our city, nation, and world are inextricably bound up together: "Seek the peace of the city where I have sent you into exile, and pray to the Lord on its behalf, for in its peace, you will find your peace" (Jer 29:7, author's translation).

And when we seek peace, we begin where we are.

The movie *Amazing Grace* depicts the life of William Wilberforce, the English abolitionist. My favorite part of the movie is the community around Wilberforce. At one point there's a montage of the community's participation in the abolitionist movement: people tell their neighbors about the horrors of the slave trade, people line up to read a memoir by a former slave, a shopkeeper puts a sign in his window saying that his establishment will not serve sugar, which was harvested by slave labor. In a dramatic moment, Wilberforce calls for the end of slavery and unfurls a petition that stretches across the parliament floor. I am struck by how Wilberforce, though his work was essential, could not have done what he did without thousands of nameless saints who made tiny, daily choices that mattered profoundly, even though they were unsung, unnoticed, and ordinary. The slave trade was crippled, and eventually outlawed, not because of a few heroes but because thousands upon thousands of peacemakers made little choices that shone, light upon tiny light, which God used to overcome darkness.

At the end of days we will hear these stories of unseen faithfulness and know the names of these men and women whose small choices, unfurled one after another like a petition, brought the end of oppression.

Each time we make a small choice toward justice, or buy fair trade, or seek to share instead of hoard, or extend mercy to those around us and kindness to those with whom we disagree, or say "I forgive you," we pass peace where we are in the ways that we can. And God can take these ordinary things and, like fish and bread, bless them and multiply them. He can make revolution stories out of smallness. He can change the world through shopkeepers who serve tea without sugar.

Our neighbor, Steven, lives in our garage apartment and is one of our best friends. He is also more like an Old Testament prophet than anyone else I know. And he's a farmer: a farmer-prophet. He's challenging and convicting and passionate and, some would say, slightly odd. He's the type who might bellow over a beer about society's decay or discuss the theological significance of spider larvae. And we love that about him.

Steven started a program, Genesis Gardens, that seeks to love and serve the homeless. He spends his days growing vegetables with homeless people in our city, cultivating hope as well as the earth, growing community among the men and women who sleep on the streets.

Steven's days look really different from mine. I hear him come and go throughout the day, on his way to do good in the world while I sit at my writing desk or change a diaper or sweep up crackers that my toddler threw on the floor.

It's easy for me to think that Steven is doing the real work of God, that he is the peacemaker, that his life and work count and give God pleasure, while I'm just sidelined. But as I have lived alongside Steven, I have found that our ordinary days turn out to be very similar—we both seek to love, we both lose patience with those closest to us, we both have moments of hope that glimmer amid the mundane. We both seek to pass the peace in our daily life and work.

And, more and more, I'm seeing that Steven's work and my work are inseparable. He needs me to seek peace with my husband. He needs us, as his friends, to pursue God and to love each other and our children well. He needs me to apologize to Jonathan for raising my voice in the argument we had today. He needs me to forgive.

And we need Steven. We need him to be the prophet he is, to never let us forget that the poor are among us. We need him to constantly expand our horizons beyond our front door. We need him to keep inviting us to volunteer with him and to tell us how to pray for him. We need him to sit at our table and not mind (or at least not mind too much) when our kids throw green beans across the room.

Last week we met Steven at the homeless shelter downtown. He'd invited us. He held my daughter's hand as she saw homelessness up close. "Why is that man sleeping on the sidewalk?" she whispered.

We need Steven so that our daughter can ask that question.

Steven tells me stories about the men and women that he works with, often stories of sadness and tragedy. He would be the first to say that the problem of poverty is not simply a lack of money.

It's a lack of community, a lack of deep ties—family, friends, people you can count on, people to catch you when you fall. I sometimes think of my work, as a wife and a mom imperfectly seeking to love those around me, as a kind of homelessness prevention program. We want our kids to learn to build community, to be peacemakers that can go into the world and bless those around them.

Sometimes Steven, Jonathan, and I sit together on our porch at night and Steven tells us about his discouragements and his passions and dreams for our city. He tells us stories of redemption, stories of the lonely finding a family. And we talk to him about our work among scholars at the university, or about potty training and sleep deprivation. In these conversations on the porch, our work in the world, big and small, is all wrapped up together. We need each other to pursue God and to seek the peace of our city.

Steven said to me once, "You and Jonathan stabilize me. And I hope to destabilize you." What he meant is that he won't let us get too comfortable. He won't let us settle into our world of kids and mortgages and family joys and squabbles, and forget that our family is part of, a microcosm of, a larger movement, the kingdom coming, the work of God to "proclaim good news to the poor . . . to proclaim liberty to the captives" (Lk 4:18). And, honestly, having our comfort challenged by our friend can be a pain in the neck. I can feel guilty. I can feel bothered. Old Testament prophets are terrible at tea parties.

But I need my friend and I need to be reminded, more than is comfortable, of the marginalized. And he needs us: young parents who are ordinary and worn out. Even though he spoke of destabilizing us, I'm steadied by the call to remain missional and to seek peace in the small ways in front of me. Steven reminds me of reality—the world is no tea party. When I get caught up in pettiness and exhaustion, I need to be reminded that my family and community are part of a larger mission. And yet I also need to remember that my small sphere, my ordinary day, matters to the mission—that the ordinary and unnoticed passing of the peace each day is part of what God is growing in and through me. It will bring a harvest, in good time.

Biblically, there is no divide between "radical" and "ordinary" believers. We are all called to be willing to follow Christ in radical ways, to answer the call of the one who told us to deny ourselves and take up our cross. And yet we are also called to stability, to the daily grind of responsibility for those nearest us, to the challenge of a mundane, well-lived Christian life. "Passing the peace" in every way we can, in the place and sphere to which God has called us, is neither a "radical" practice nor an "ordinary" practice; it is merely a Christian practice, one that each of us must inhabit daily. We can become far too comfortable with the American status quo, and we need prophetic voices that challenge us to follow our radical, comfort-afflicting Redeemer. But we must also learn to follow Jesus in this workaday world of raising kids, caring for our neighbors, budgeting, doing laundry, and living our days responsibly with stability, generosity, and faithfulness.

> **Biblically, there is no divide between
> "radical" and "ordinary" believers.**

Steven is getting married in a few months, and I, as his friend and sister in Christ, need him to be a peacemaker in his marriage.

I'm officiating his wedding, and I will exhort him to seek peace in his new home as ardently as he does among those who are homeless, because the way he will treat his wife, behind closed doors and in the patterns of their life together, is as important in the kingdom as his work on the streets. These are his ways of seeking shalom.

But today, I blew it. I lost patience with my husband. I spoke sarcastically. I honestly didn't care much about peace.

After twenty minutes of playing chicken, we cave. I apologize; he does too. We forgive each other. Dropping my sword and walking into the next room to apologize felt like a kind of dying. It smarted.

We'll have to keep forgiving all day, every time we think back to our argument, every time we're tempted to pick up the sword again. Peace takes a whole lot of work. Conflict and resentment seem to be the easier route. Shorter, anyway. Less humiliating.

Anne Lamott writes that we learn the practice of reconciliation by starting with those nearest us. "Earth is Forgiveness School. You might as well start at the dinner table. That way, you can do this work in comfortable pants."[7]

Because we are broken people in a broken world, seeking shalom always involves forgiveness and reconciliation. Paul tells the Corinthians that "Christ reconciled us to himself and gave us the ministry of reconciliation; that is, in Christ God was reconciling the world to himself, not counting their trespasses against them, and entrusting to us the message of reconciliation" (2 Cor 5:18-19). This is not easy. Today's small spat in the kitchen was minor, but there are hurts in relationships—even patterns of hurt—that go deep. In those deep places, forgiveness and reconciliation cost us. We have to struggle long and hard for it, through time and tears. The truth we enact each week when we pass the peace with those worshiping around us is, at times, a hard truth, a truth that smarts.

On the night before his crucifixion, Jesus knelt down and washed his disciples' feet, even the feet of those he knew would soon deny him. It will cost us something to be about this ministry of reconciliation—even in our kitchens, even in comfy pants. When we have been wounded by those around us, extending forgiveness— "not counting their trespasses against them"—is giving up our right to recompense, to resentment, to self-righteousness.

In the Anglican liturgy the passing of the peace comes after confession and absolution, on the heels of our reminder that we are forgiven. This too is no coincidence. Our forgiveness and reconciliation flow from Christ's forgiveness of us. Out of gratitude over the enormous debt our king has forgiven, we forgive our debtors. Receiving God's gift of reconciliation enables us to give and receive reconciliation with those around us.

In the end, God is the peacemaker. It is not simply "peace" that we pass to each other. It is the peace of Christ, the peace of our peacemaker. Christ's peace is never a cheap peace. It is never a peace that skims the surface or papers over the wrong that's been done. It is not a peace that plays nicey-nice, denies hurt, or avoids conflict. It is never a peace that is insincere or ignores injustice. It's a peace that is honest and hard-won, that speaks truth and seeks justice, that costs something, and that takes time. It is a peace that offers reconciliation.

We cannot seek peace out of our own strength. We all blow it—we fail those around us, we pass judgment instead, we retreat into selfishness as often as we extend a hand. If we are ever peace-makers, it is not without a good deal of war within our hearts.

But God has reconciled us to himself, and he brings reconcili-ation and peace to every sphere of life. He is bringing peace to city streets and out in the wilderness and on farms and in the suburbs and in my kitchen. He is reconciling us to himself, to each other, and to the earth.

God's ministry of reconciliation works its way into all of life, even into these small moments of our day.

In the end, this practice each Sunday—the passing of peace—is a prayer. We are asking that God would do something we cannot, so that we can extend peace, not of our own making, but of Christ's, our Reconciler.

We are quarreling people, but God is reforming us to be people who, through our ordinary moments, establish his kingdom of peace. Believing this is an act of a faith. It takes faith to believe that our little, frail faithfulness can produce fruit. It takes faith to believe that laying down my sword in my kitchen has anything to do with cosmic peace on earth. And it takes faith to believe that God is making us into people—slowly, through repentance—who are capable of saying to the world through our lives, "Peace of Christ to you."

7

checking email

blessing and sending

I open my inbox to a swirling mass of tasks I need to complete, people I need to respond to, and things that call for my time: a plea for volunteers from my daughter's teacher, forms to complete for my supervisor, a smattering of people with whom I need to set up meetings, an Evite, a note from my mom, an old friend who's traveling through and wants to sleep on my couch, an appointment reminder from our doctor's office, and a few mass emails, mainly charities asking for donations or listservs I'm on for my job.

My brain cannot take in the sheer volume of email, the number of people needing a response, the sorting, deciding, writing, and deleting that lies before me. My eyes glaze over. I want to escape—to go elsewhere online or to back away from the computer in relieved defeat—bested, once again, by my nemesis.

I know people who empty their inbox every day. Those people have superpowers and exist on cheerfulness and productivity as food. They've given me books on how to be more efficient and organized with email, and I've read parts of them. But I still have unopened Groupon deals from four years ago.

There are days when I try to catch up, when I seem to gain a little ground on the hamster wheel, but I've never been able to master this task. Mostly because I don't like it and therefore I avoid it. I'm fairly certain that one day there will be three numbers engraved on my tombstone as a legacy and a warning: my birth date, my death date, and the number of unopened emails still awaiting a response in my inbox.

◆ ◆ ◆

At the end of our worship service each week, we are blessed and sent out into the world. We have fed on Word and sacrament and now we are released into the wild. In the *Book of Common Prayer* there is a prayer that is sometimes called the "prayer after communion" or the "prayer for mission" that we say together each Sunday: "And now, Father, send us out to do the work you have given us to do, to love and serve you as faithful witnesses of Christ our Lord . . ." At the conclusion of our time together, we receive benediction and are told to go: "Let us go forth in the name of Christ," or "Go in peace to love and serve the Lord."[1]

We are blessed and sent.

There is no competition between the work we do as a people in gathered worship—*liturgy* means "the work of the people"—and our vocations in the world. For believers, the two are intrinsically part of one another.

In recent years evangelical leaders and churches have increasingly focused on integrating faith and work. This effort is both needed and immensely helpful.[2] But many of us still struggle with the temptation to divide our "secular" work from our "spiritual" lives and wonder whether we can fully participate in Jesus' mission with our particular training, gifts, and vocations. This is true not only of professionals but of stay-at-home moms and students and blue-collar workers. We wonder, *What does worship have to do with my work?*

It is not that supposedly spiritual activities like evangelism, prayer, or gathered worship are our real or important duties, while daily work is inferior. Nor, however, is it that the nitty-gritty of our workaday world is our real work and our spiritual lives and Sunday worship are add-ons, a sometimes awkward insertion of devotion and moral teaching in our otherwise hard-boiled, pragmatic lives. The work we do together each week in gathered worship transforms and sends us into the work we do in our homes and offices. Likewise, our professional and vocational work is part of the mission and meaning of our gathered worship. We are people who are blessed and sent; this identity transforms how we embody work and worship in the world, in our week, even in our small day.

We often understand the Protestant Reformation as a conflict about doctrine. Justification. Grace versus works. Ecclesiology. Indulgences. And it was. But what captured the imagination of the commoners in Europe during the Reformation was not only the finer points of doctrine, but the earthy notion of vocation.[3] The idea that all good work is holy work was revolutionary. The Reformation toppled a vocational hierarchy that had placed monks, nuns, and priests at the top and everyone else below. The Reformers taught that a farmer may worship God by being a good farmer and that a parent changing diapers could be as near to Jesus as the pope. This was a scandal.

Even now, often subconsciously, we tend to rate some jobs as holier or more spiritual than others. Whether we place missionaries, social activists, artists, the rich, the powerful, the famous, or the hypereducated at the top, we tend to value certain types of work above others.

In his book *Every Good Endeavor*, Tim Keller outlines what various Christian communities emphasize and teach about how to serve God at work. He says that we receive different (and conflicting) messages about work. We're told that the main way to serve God in our work is by being personally honest and evangelizing our coworkers. Or by furthering social justice. Or by simply doing excellent and skillful work. Or by creating beauty. Or by working from a Christian motivation to glorify God by impacting culture. Or by having a "grateful, joyful, gospel-changed heart." Or by doing whatever gives you the greatest sense of satisfaction. Or by making as much money as possible and being generous.[4] All of these may be important ways to serve God through our work but, since it is not possible to live out of every one of these messages simultaneously, Christians either tend to be confused about exactly how their work matters to God and to the church or they pick one or two main emphases and judge those who aren't living up to their particular take on meaningful work.

I grew up feeling like ministry was the most important, most spiritual work. But in my current context, most people I know (and the students I've worked with) don't think they need to quit their jobs or graduate school to be in "full-time ministry." Many, however, do feel guilty if their work does not clearly and directly impact the poor. Over the past couple of decades evangelicals have grown in concern for issues of social justice, which is a welcome and needed corrective to an unbiblical separation of the gospel from social concern.[5] But now we can inadvertently elevate "world-changing" jobs and denigrate others. Recently a friend of mine who is preparing to be a professor went to an evangelical conference and left feeling like the only jobs that mattered were "radical" jobs working directly among the poor and marginalized. He told me that it seemed like "the rest of us just had jobs to fund that important work." He wondered aloud, "How could anyone leave that conference with a sense of calling outside of a few sanctified careers?"

But God cares about my friend's work and his research, and not solely as a means to an end. The Christian faith teaches that all work that is not immoral or unethical is part of God's kingdom mission.

The kingdom of God comes both through our gathered worship each week and our "scattered" worship in our work each day. Thus all work, even a simple, small task, matters eternally. Author Steve Garber challenges any attempt to compartmentalize worship from work with the credo for The Washington Institute for Faith, Vocation, and Culture: "Vocation is integral, not incidental, to the Missio Dei."[6]

The *missio Dei*, the mission of God (it could also be translated "the sending of God")—the idea that every part of creation will be redeemed and rightly ordered around worship of the Trinity—is manifest in an integral way in our work.

◆◆◆

Each week when we gather for worship we enact again the reality that we are blessed and sent. At times, this big vision of the *missio Dei* can make its way, very obviously, into our mission and purpose statement, our life goals and vision, but it can easily get lost in the daily grind. For me, being a "blessed and sent" one on God's mission seems distant and inscrutable in the annoying task of email. Yet each message in my inbox, in some way, touches on my vocation, or rather, vocations. Each email has to do with my professional, family, and civic life.

This kingdom vision—our identity as those blessed and sent—must work itself out in the small routines of our daily work and vocation, as we go to meetings, check our email, make our children dinner, or mow the lawn.

I have a friend who is a high-up leader in a national organization. He's doing good work and making an impact through his career. But when you ask him what he does for a living, he answers, "If you ask my kids, they'd tell you that I check emails and go to meetings." This kingdom vision—our identity as those blessed and sent—must work itself out in the small routines of our daily work and vocation, as we go to meetings, check our email, make our children dinner, or mow the lawn.

It's easy for me to assume that the parts of my vocation that God cares about are the parts that I like. The rest is the dross and doldrums and groaning and necessary evils. Luther said, "God himself will milk the cows through him whose vocation it is."[7] But could God himself check email through me? Could he balance the family budget and fold the laundry through me? Could he fill out bureaucratic work forms through me? Does he care about any of this?

The Puritans, who talked more about work and vocation than almost any community before or since, articulated a helpful idea that Eugene Peterson later termed "vocational holiness."[8] The idea is that we are sanctified—made holy—not in the abstract but through our concrete vocation. Christian holiness is not a free-floating goodness removed from the world, a few feet above the ground. It is specific and, in some sense, tailored to who we particularly are. We grow in holiness in the honing of our specific vocation. We can't be holy in the abstract. Instead we become a holy blacksmith or a holy mother or a holy physician or a holy systems analyst. We seek God in and through our particular vocation and place in life.

Each kind of work is therefore its own kind of craft that must be developed over time, both for our own sanctification and for the good of the community. As we seek to do our work well and hone our craft, we are developed and honed in our work. Our task is not to somehow inject God into our work but to join God in the work he is already doing in and through our vocational lives. Therefore, holiness itself is something like a craft—not an abstract state to which we ascend but an earthy wisdom and love that is part and parcel of how we spend our day.

We learn the craft of holiness day by day in the living of a particular life. The *missio Dei* is lived out, not primarily in my theological reflections on the importance of motherhood (though that does matter), but as I hone the craft of motherhood in small moments when I'm weary and frazzled and kneel down on my kitchen floor to listen to a crying child.

My identity as one who is "blessed and sent" must be embraced and enfleshed, even in these hours of email as I seek to form better habits of responsibility and discipline. These are the small tasks in which we live out God's blessing and into which we are sent; we are blessed and sent into the real ways that we spend our hours. Garber says,

> In the daily rhythms for everyone everywhere, we live our lives in the marketplaces of this world: in homes and neighborhoods, in schools and on farms, in hospitals and businesses, and our vocations are bound up with the ordinary work that ordinary people do. We are not great shots across the bow of history; rather, by simple grace, we are hints of hope.[9]

We are fed in worship, blessed, and sent out to be "hints of hope" (a phrase Garber borrows from Walker Percy). We are part of God's big vision and mission—the redemption of all things—through the earthy craft of living out our vocation, hour by hour, task by task. I want to do the big work of the kingdom, but I have to learn to live it out in the small tasks before me—the *missio Dei* in the daily grind.

> **These are the small tasks in which we live out God's blessing and into which we are sent; we are blessed and sent into the real ways that we spend our hours.**

The idea of vocational holiness is easier for me to embrace in the imagined context of a Puritan village—amid farmers, cheese makers, preachers, and blacksmiths—than in the context of my actual day in a city full of tech companies, office parks, and drive-throughs.

To begin with, there's a clear artistry in blacksmithing and cheese making that is, at first glance, absent in much of our work in the contemporary world. Though I acknowledge the darker side of Puritan communities, for me, a Puritan village has a romantic appeal. It seems quaint with its butchers, bakers, and candlestick makers. It is much harder for me to see the holiness, dignity, and artistry inherent in financial planning or office administration or retail sales or bus driving or burger flipping.

A Puritan carpenter could make a chair, stand back, gaze at a job well done, and sell it to his neighbor who he'd known for decades, knowing that his neighbor would be blessed by many hours in his good chair. There is far more abstraction and intangibility in our jobs now than when the Puritans sermonized on vocational holiness. There are global, systemic forces that can make work in the modern world dehumanizing and vicious (*vicious* means "prone to vice"). The song "Sprawl II" by Arcade Fire is a screed against these forces in modernity, where "dead shopping malls rise like mountains beyond mountains." The song continues, "They heard me singing and they told me to stop / Quit these pretentious things and just punch the clock / These days my life, I feel it has no purpose."[10]

There can be a deep sense of purposelessness in modern work, in our day in and day out punching the clock. We live in a world where I can sit at my desk and email people I've never met in order to discuss work that I will do by staring at a screen. And though we must fight against the injustice and inhumane conditions that can make modern work intolerable, we must not inadvertently create a new "hierarchy of holiness" that elevates ancient work above our modern jobs. Part of our particular task as believers sent out by the church for the *missio Dei* is to learn to embody holiness, not only in blacksmithing or cheese making, but in and through work that is inevitably shaped by modernity and technology. I have to check my email. In this hour, that is the work that God has given me to do.

Most of us are not called to simply abandon the modern world for a back-to-nature ideal. Instead, even now, we must hone the crafts and habits that allow us to work well and to love our neighbors through our work, whether that neighbor is someone I've known for decades or someone sitting at a computer screen far away. I have been blessed and helped by people who do modern work well, people who have served me, their neighbor, through what Keller calls the "ministry of competence."[11]

Here's the thing: I hate email. Email makes me feel like I am a failure who can't get her life together. Yet emailing is a holy task. Part of my sanctification and part of the world's redemption is for me to learn to do my work well—or at least better than I currently do it.

I've had a lot of different jobs, all of which have formed me in the craft of holiness. Mom, priest, campus minister, writer. I've worked at a bookstore, a coffee shop, an organic grocery store, an elementary school office, and a drug rehab center. I've been on a film crew, taught English overseas, assisted in kids' ballroom dancing classes, and nannied. My least favorite job was working in a giant medical complex as an appointment scheduler. It was a year of fluorescent lights, headsets, an aching back from hours of sitting, angry patients arguing with me about their HMOs, and long afternoons counting down the minutes until five o'clock. My days were spent staring at a screen taking call after call for eight hours—completely uncreative, tedious work. And what made it harder was that my coworkers were often hot-tempered and disagreeable.

But then there was Dee. Dee had been on the job for a long time and she was great at it. She beamed with pride over the family photos that decorated her desk. She knew how to tell which patients really needed urgent care and which were simply being impatient. She remained calm and helped soothe flustered or angry patients. She was good with details (and we had to cover a lot of details), and she seemed to be friends with everyone in the office.

Even in a mechanized and robotic environment in a soulless, stressful office, Dee demonstrated excellence—she honed her craft. Her job (like mine) may have seemed like the most menial in our medical facility, but she did it well, and in so doing she made my work life better and kept the place running. She was an agent of redemption.

◆ ◆ ◆

Our Puritan craftsman could make a good chair and then leave it behind and move on to other tasks, rest, or be with friends. He did not face a culture of workaholism fed by a 24/7 world of connection and productivity. He did not have a smartphone. In our modern-day society, when we are blessed and sent to go do the work God has given us to do, we are sent into a culture where work can become all-consuming and boundless.

Our frantic work lives are disconnected from the rhythms of the seasons or day and night. We can work constantly. I can check my email twenty-four hours a day, rain or shine. We can feel like we are always at work, since work can follow us everywhere we go. With these changes come an increased temptation to make work and productivity an idol to which we'll sacrifice rest, health, and relationships.

What might vocational holiness look like when technology can breed habits that feed an unhealthy and ungodly appetite for endless productivity? Like Martha, we can get too caught up in the kitchen, "anxious and troubled about many things" (Lk 10:41). It's easy to be anxious and exhausted and miss the greater thing, especially when work is always at hand—literally, in our handheld device.

At the opposite extreme of workaholism, I can idealize and exalt escapism into a contemplative ideal. Even though I'd confess with the Reformers that a farmer's work in a field is every bit as important and holy as a monk's work in his cell, when it comes to my own mundane work I often want to escape to the monastic cell.

Whether it comes from my youth group drilling into me the importance of a daily quiet time, or my deep respect for monasticism and contemplative spirituality, I still imagine "meeting God" in a silent place, preferably outdoors by the ocean or a still pond, or in a cathedral with stained glass, with my Bible and journal and hours of stillness. That's how I prefer God to meet me, not through a "ministry of competence" in checking my email. This longing for a contemplative ideal can be a particular burden for me as a young mom, in a home that is typically loud, active, sleepless, and filled with unending requests and needs.

I need a third way—neither frantic activity nor escape from the workaday world, a way of working that is shaped by being blessed and sent. This third way is marked by freedom from compulsion and anxiety because it is rooted in benediction—God's blessing and love. But it also actively embraces God's mission in the world into which we are sent.

A fourteenth-century monk, Walter Hilton, wrote letters to a layman involved in commercial and political life who wanted to enter contemplative life in a religious community. Hilton challenged this man to stay in his profession and to embrace "a third way, a mixed life combining the activity of Martha with the reflectiveness of Mary." Hilton concluded that "such a spirituality needs to be consciously modeled and taught."[12]

This third way avoids the frenzied workaholism that arises from our attempts to earn our own blessedness and steer our own destinies. And yet it doesn't abandon our daily tasks, nor does it devalue them as less holy.

B. B. Warfield, a professor of theology at Princeton in the late nineteenth and early twentieth centuries, was concerned about what he saw as a "tendency . . . to restless activity" at the expense of spiritual depth.[13] Warfield reminds us that "activity, of course, is good. . . . But not when it is substituted for inner religious strength. We cannot get along without our Marthas. But what shall we do when, through all the length and breadth of the land, we shall search in vain for a Mary?"[14] Yet, in the same address, Warfield integrates the value of prayer and stillness with his vocation as an academic. He counters the charge that "ten minutes on your knees will give you a truer, deeper, more operative knowledge of God than ten hours over your books" by saying that a right understanding of his vocation would lead to "ten hours over your books, on your knees."[15]

I want to learn how to spend time over my inbox, laundry, and tax forms, yet, mysteriously, always on my knees, offering up my work as a prayer to the God who blesses and sends.

Living a third way of work—where we seek vocational holiness in and through our work even as we resist the idolatry of work and accomplishment—allows us to live with work as a form of prayer. This entwining of work and prayer is part of ancient spiritual practice. Long before the Puritans or B. B. Warfield, the Latin phrase *ora et labora*, or "pray and work," marked monastic spirituality, particularly in Benedictine communities. The idea is perhaps most famously embodied by Brother Lawrence, who wrote, "The time of business does not with me differ from the time of prayer, and in the noise and clatter of my kitchen . . . I possess God in as great tranquility as if I were upon my knees at the blessed sacrament."[16]

It is hard for me to believe that checking email could ever be a place of prayer. I want God to call me to other things, things that feel more important, meaningful, and thrilling. But this work, in this hour, is a living prayer that I may "go in peace to love and serve the Lord."[17]

That doesn't mean I have to be giddy about checking email. I'm not sure I ever will be. But I want to remember that we were made for a day when God's chosen people will "long enjoy the work of their hands" (Is 65:22). We are blessed and sent to work in this world, where we will face fallenness and toil. But even still our labor is not in vain. And one day all of it, even our smallest daily tasks— even email—will be sifted and sorted and redeemed.

8

sitting in traffic

liturgical time and an unhurried God

I'm on the highway, Interstate 35. Stopped.

I can't see what's ahead. Is there a wreck? Road construction? I check my map app. A thick red line stretches on for what appears to be over a mile.

I'm going to be here a while.

My kids are strapped into their car seats kicking the seats in front of them in boredom. We are all a little tired and a little whiny. It's hot in the car. I crank up the air conditioning and turn on NPR.

We need to get home soon or my kids will be cranky—"starving," they'll say. They'll get a late bath and be late for bed, and there goes my hope of a little downtime. As I wait, I grow increasingly irritated.

I've never really understood why people honk in traffic. No one can go any faster. We're all stuck. No one's particularly happy about it. But people honk, as if to shake a sonic fist at the sky. In the face of our powerlessness, our stuckness, our mortal minutes counting down, we just honk: an act of rage and protest that only adds noise, not movement. We're geese, caught in a trap, honking.

I judge the people who honk in traffic, but if my feelings made sounds they'd be honking too. I am impatient. I live in an instant world where I like to think I am the captain of the clock. I live with the illusion that time—my time at least—is something I control. I am not a farmer. I don't have to wait for harvest or for the weather to change. I'm not a midwife. I don't have to wait for babies to come. When my computer moves too slowly—seconds really—I murmur, "This is taking forever."

Of course, if I knew how long I have left to live, if the length of my remaining days or those of someone close to me could be counted in weeks, I'd understand that time is not in my control. Or if I lived without the luxury of electricity, time would more obviously call the shots.

But in my life, time is most often something I seek to manage, or something I resent—something, it seems, that I never have enough of. In my frenetic life, I forget how to slow down and wait.

For the good of my own soul I need to feel what it's like to wait, to let the moments march past. And here I am, plunged into an ancient spiritual practice in the middle of the freeway—forced, against my will, to practice waiting.

———

One of my favorite scenes in literature is when the Lilliputians in *Gulliver's Travels* think that, because Gulliver keeps checking his clock, it must be his god.[1] It was Swift's clever commentary on his era's worship of time, hurry, and efficiency, which applies just as easily to us today. (By the Lilliputians' logic, my god is my smartphone.)

But the reality is that I do not control time. Every day I wait. I wait for help, for healing, for days to come, for rescue and redemption. And like all of us, I'm waiting to die.

And I wait for glory, for the coming King, for the resurrection of the body.

Christians are people who wait. We live in liminal time, in the already and not yet. Christ has come, and he will come again. We dwell in the meantime. We wait.

But in my daily life I've developed habits of impatience—of speeding ahead, of trying to squeeze more into my cluttered day. How can I live as one who watches and waits for the coming kingdom when I can barely wait for water to boil?

Theologian Hans Urs von Balthasar suggests that impatience is at the root of all sin. He explains the central role of patience in the Christian life:

> God intended man to have all good, but in . . . God's time; and therefore all disobedience, all sin, consists essentially in breaking out of time. Hence the restoration of order by the Son of God had to be the annulment of that premature snatching at knowledge, the beating down of the hand outstretched toward eternity, the repentant return from a false, swift transfer of eternity to a true, slow confinement in time. . . . Patience [is] the basic constituent of Christianity . . . the power to wait, to persevere, to hold out, to endure to the end, not to transcend one's own limitations, not to force issues by playing the hero or the titan, but to practice the virtue that lies beyond heroism, the meekness of the lamb which is led.[2]

As one who is beloved of God, I must learn the hard practice of patience.

Sitting in traffic, stuck, is one of very few times in my day where I embody the true state of my whole human existence—on the way, already but not yet, living as a creature in the in-between, waiting.

— ◆ —

Christians exist in an alternative chronology. The church has its own time.

I didn't make this discovery until college, and it left me dazzled. I was like a kid discovering a secret passageway in my own house. Liturgical time—"You mean this has been here all along? Right in my house? Ready to be explored?"

I had long felt that I couldn't get the hang of living in time. Growing up, I resisted it. I always dawdled, which irritated my very punctual father. I was too slow, never on time, never in a hurry. I did not know how to live as if time were a limited resource.

As I grew older, I felt like time had no shape or meaning. I think part of my discomfort with the concept of time was that I lived in central Texas, where leaves don't change with the seasons and it only snows once every decade or so. I craved meaning, rhythm, and boundaries in time, but these were not immediately apparent in the environment around me.

Texans try to follow the rest of America and keep up a façade of the seasons. We'd stake life-size wooden snowmen into the ground in front of our house at Christmastime. Wooden snowmen! Real snowmen were nowhere to found, so we used wooden ones to perpetuate the myth of seasonal change in the midst of sixty-degree weather. It seemed hokey to me, even as a kid. So time itself seemed artificial and trumped up. Human-made time might remind us of something real, but mostly it was a product, an invention made to sell something. Maybe to sell snowmen to Southerners.

Discovering the liturgical calendar felt like discovering real time. It gave a transcendent shape to my life. Time was no longer arbitrary—an academic calendar, a marketing ploy, a back to school sale, a Labor Day blowout, a national holiday, a sports season. Now time was sacred. It was structured by worship. It marked the church as a global, alternative people. Time had shape and meaning. All of a sudden, time was a story. And I could live in a story.

Human-made time might remind us of something real, but mostly it was a product, an invention made to sell something. Maybe to sell snowmen to Southerners.

In the church calendar we learn the rhythm of life through narrative. Every week we reenact God's creative work and rest. Every year we retell the story of Jesus. Advent, Christmas, Epiphany: the story of God's people longing for a Messiah, Christ's birth, and then, slowly, his revelation as a King to all the world. Lent, Easter, Pentecost: the story of Christ's temptation, life in a fallen world, suffering, death, resurrection, and ascension, and then the coming of the Holy Spirit and the birth of the church. We live this story every year, week by week, living out what we confess in the creed in the way we name our days.

And in liturgical time, we make space—lots of space—for waiting.

When we practice the Sabbath, we not only look back to God's rest after his work of creation but we look forward to the rest ahead, to the Sabbath to come when God will finish his work of re-creation. We recall together that we are waiting for the end of the story, for all things to be made new.

In the liturgical year there is never celebration without preparation. First we wait, we mourn, we ache, we repent. We aren't ready to celebrate until we acknowledge, over time through ritual and worship, that we and this world are not yet right and whole.[3] Before Easter, we have Lent. Before Christmas, we have Advent. We fast. Then we feast.

We prepare. We practice waiting.

In the sacred rhythm of our time, we embrace the tension of our reality. We live between D-day and V-day. The victory is secured, but the war continues a little longer.

We are impatient people. We want happiness now. Fulfillment and gratification now. Time is just another commodity that we seek to maximize.

I get angry in traffic because it reminds me that time is not at my bidding.

In her book *Receiving the Day* Dorothy Bass describes how perceiving time as something that we own and manage—as blocks in a day planner—can drive us to the false belief that time is primarily a force to be tamed, used, and controlled.

Bass describes me with stinging accuracy:

> We delude ourselves into believing that if we can just get everything done, if we can only tie up all the loose ends, if we can even once get ahead of the crush, we will prove our worth and establish ourselves in safety. Our problem with time is social, cultural, and economic, to be sure. But it is also a spiritual problem, one that

runs right to the core of who we are as human beings. . . . Indeed, these distortions drive us into the arms of a false theology: we come to believe that we, not God, are the masters of time. We come to believe that our worth must be proved by the way we spend our hours and that our ultimate safety depends on our own good management.[4]

The reality is that time is a stream we are swept into. Time is a gift from God, a means of worship. I need the church to remind me of reality: time is not a commodity that I control, manage, or consume. The practice of liturgical time teaches me, day by day, that time is not mine. It does not revolve around me. Time revolves around God—what he has done, what he is doing, and what he will do.

We live in a waiting world, a world where time itself, along with all of creation, groans in childbirth, waiting for something to be born. Here in traffic, when I'm stuck in the in-between, neither where I've come from nor yet where I'm going, I inhabit the liturgical rhythm I practice year after year: waiting and hoping. My present reality is fundamentally oriented toward what is to come. I am on the way.

Waiting, therefore, is an act of faith in that it is oriented toward the future. Yet our assurance of hope is rooted in the past, in the person of Jesus of Nazareth and in his promises and resurrection. In this way, waiting, like time itself, centers on Christ—the fulcrum of time.

—◆◆◆—

Because of Christ's work, we wait with expectation. We replace the despair that the passing of time inevitably brings—"ashes to ashes, dust to dust"—with faith—"if we have died with him, we shall also live with him."[5] The rhythms of the church calendar orient us to our truest future. Our imaginations are fixed on what is to come, on the future glory when God will set all things right.

Practicing the liturgical calendar is a counterformation to a culture of impatience. It sets us apart as a peculiar people who resist what James K. A. Smith calls "the incessant 24/7-ness of our frenetic commercial culture."[6]

> **In the midst of our culture's tendency to embrace constant revelry that leaves us feeling hung-over and empty, we are people in training, together learning to wait.**

Scripture tells us that when we "hope for what we do not see, we wait for it with patience" (Rom 8:25). We live each ordinary day in the light of a future reality. Our best life is still to come.

Practicing the church's time sets us at odds with the world's time. Our culture tends to rush from celebration to celebration—from a month of Halloween to two months of Christmas to the Super Bowl, Mardi Gras, Cinco De Mayo, and on and on. In the midst of our culture's tendency to embrace constant revelry that leaves us feeling hung-over and empty, we are people in training, together learning to wait. We practice ways of waiting, hoping, slowing down, preparing, and—because of all that—truly celebrating.

I spent my first summer out of college with a community of Christians who worked among homeless teenagers and abused kids. The darkness that these friends confronted daily was almost palpable. Every week we encountered suicide, violence, the ravages of addiction, and generations of neglect and abuse. Yet that

Christian community, more than any other I've seen, celebrated wholeheartedly and with intense joy. When someone had a birthday, it was an all-day game of happy surprises. When one of the kids they worked with reached a milestone—a month of sobriety or new growth in healing—they pulled out all the stops. They lived so close to profound pain and yet, in the midst of mourning, they learned to practice celebration. They lived in waiting and celebrated each mile marker. It was a laughter born of their long labor.

❖ ❖ ❖

I have a framed print above my bed of a painting by my friend Jan, who has learned much about waiting through long and painful practice. She has had recurring cancer and significant health problems that have given her scars and a hard-won joy. She's been shaped through waiting—waiting for a call from the doctor, for test results to come back, for another treatment, for healing, for she's not sure what. Her home is filled with her paintings, and one day as I walked in I was drawn to one in particular. It was abstract, luminous, and intricately textured, and there was a keyhole etched on the canvas. Standing before it I felt like I was standing before an unearthly, mysterious door. I turned to Jan and said, "I want to see what's on the other side of the door." She smiled and said, "Good. That's exactly how I wanted you to feel."

The painting is called "The Gift." She'd painted it during a time when she was struggling to remain faithful as she waited and waited and waited. She explained that she wanted the viewer to have that stretching sense of waiting, of not being able to glimpse what was on the other side, suspended in a posture of expectation and uncertainty. She looked at me and said, "I always felt like I was waiting for the gift. But I've come to see that the waiting is the gift."[7]

What did that mean? For me, standing before that door was maddening. And yet Jan, who had practiced waiting far longer and better than I, knew what it was like to wait patiently, believing that God's timing is perfect and that, mysteriously, there is more happening while we wait than just waiting. In waiting God has met Jan and sown in her things that only grow with time—with changing seasons and bated breath.

God is at work in us and through us as we wait. Our waiting is active and purposeful. My friend Steven, the farmer-prophet, reminds me that a fallow field is never dormant. As dirt sits waiting for things to be planted and grown, there is work being done invisibly and silently. Microorganisms are breeding, moving, and eating. Wind and sun and fungi and insects are dancing a delicate dance that leavens the soil, making it richer and better, readying it for planting.

Robert Wilken highlights the relationship between patience and hope in his exploration of the early church father Tertullian.

> The singular mark of patience is not endurance or fortitude but hope. To be impatient . . . is to live without hope. Patience is grounded in the Resurrection. It is life oriented toward a future that is God's doing, and its sign is longing, not so much to be released from the ills of the present, but in anticipation of the good to come.[8]

Even now as we wait, God is bringing the kingdom that will one day be fully known. We can be as patient as a fallow field because we know there are gifts promised by a Giver who can be trusted.

Yet our patience does not make us passive about the brokenness of the world. We are not blithely waiting to abandon this world for another. Christian faith is never an otherworldly, pie-in-the-sky sentimentality that ignores the injustice and darkness around us. We know that things are not as they should be. We also know that here—not up in the sky, but in this earthy, waiting world of peach trees and inchworms, of brass bands and didgeridoos—things will be made right. Heaven will be established right here in our midst.

Part of my impatience on I-35 is that I am unhappy with the way things are. Last week, as I waited for a haircut, the hipsters who worked at the salon handed me a beer, gave me a comfy chair, and played good music, so I didn't mind waiting so much. But here, under an overpass, surrounded by concrete, billboards with crumbling ads for McDonald's, and my wiggling kids demanding that I turn off the radio, I just want to get on with it. Come, Lord Jesus.

Christians are marked not only by patience, but also by longing. We are oriented to our future hope, yet we do not try to escape from our present reality, from the real and pressing brokenness and suffering in the world. As Smith puts it, we "will always sit somewhat uneasy in the present, haunted by the brokenness of the 'now.' The future we hope for—a future when justice rolls down like waters and righteousness like an ever-flowing stream—hangs over our present and gives us a vision of what to work for in the here and now as we continue to pray, 'Your kingdom come.'"[9]

We live in a brutal world. But in the life of Christ and the work of the Holy Spirit we glimpse redemption and participate in it. We have a telos as we wait, an ultimate purpose and aim. Because we have a telos—a kingdom where peace will reign and where God is worshiped—we can never wrap our lives in little luxuries and petty comforts and so numb ourselves to God's prophetic call for justice and wholeness in this world. Our hope for a future of shalom motivates us to press toward that reality, even in our ordinary days. Our work, our times in prayer and service, our small days lived graciously, missionally, and faithfully will bear fruit that we can't yet see.

What if, in traffic on I-35, we travelers forgot our telos? What if we all forsook our destinations—our commitment to where we are going—and came to believe that this grimy interstate was all there is? What if we all left our cars and set up cots on a dingy stretch of highway? Someone pulls a grill out of a truckbed and starts a barbecue. Maybe we set up a poker game. We aren't going anywhere. Eventually we say, "There's nowhere to go," and simply make ourselves as comfortable as we can. People begin to hoard food. Fights break out. People siphon gas and squabble over jumper cables to keep the air conditioning going. We each stake out our own territory and try to eke out an existence on the interstate, believing that these gasoline fumes and concrete pillars are all there is; this is the way the world always has been and always will be.

It would be a disaster. Out of touch with larger reality, we would have lost our telos. We'd have forgotten that there are better ways to live.

The future orientation of Christian time reminds us that we are people on the way. It allows us to live in the present as an alternative people, patiently waiting for what is to come, but never giving up on our telos. We are never quite comfortable. We seek justice, practice mercy, and herald the kingdom to come.

The liturgical calendar reminds us that we are people who live by a different story. And not just by a story, but *in* a story. God is redeeming all things, and our lives—even our days—are part of that redemption. We live in the truth that, however slowly or quickly we may be traveling, we are going somewhere. Or, more accurately, somewhere (and Someone) is drawing near to us.

Redemption is crashing into our little stretch of the universe, bit by bit, day by day, mile by coming mile. We have hope because our Lord has promised that he is preparing a place for us. We are waiting, but we will make it home.

9

calling a friend

congregation and community

After dinner, dishes, and the arduous process of putting the kids to bed, everything starts to quiet down, and I call my friend Rebekka. I leave a message, a long rambling message about highs and lows of my week. She will call back. And she'll express sympathy and talk about her day or share a disappointment or tell me how her studio opening went.

Rebekka is what Madeline L'Engle called a "friend of my right hand."[1] She's the kind of friend—one of just a handful—whose life has become so bundled up with mine that I can't make sense of me without her. She knows me, good and bad. We share a passion for beauty, butter, and urban design, and an indulgence for chips and TV, which we enjoyed together every Wednesday night when we lived on the same street. We love each other.

Two years ago I moved states and, to our great sadness, we had to say goodbye. So we visit. And in the meantime we call, in our spare minutes, in our going out and coming in.

My calls to Rebekka have become a sort of confessional booth, a place I go to spill out struggles, worries, failures, and doubts, and to celebrate hopes, joys, and successes, to ask for prayer or how to make better bone broth.

Rebekka is a professional artist. She finds beauty in everything—even in me. Her delight in me gives me hope that in my murky, mixed-up soul there remains a burning loveliness that only God could have placed there, and that he is cultivating. For years now, she and I, together with other close friends, have grappled with the gospel in the warp and woof of our daily lives. She helps me to believe.

◆ ◆ ◆

I like the parts of the worship service when we talk to each other. In historic liturgy this happens most often through the responsive reading of the Scriptures and responsive prayers. In my church we read the Psalms responsively every week. Instead of just one person reading to everyone else (a good practice in its own right), we read together, in turns. Back and forth, we share the same sacred sentences. As we join together in responsive prayer or reading, I look at the faces in the congregation: some rapt, some bored, some pained, many weary. We made it through another week. We are being the church, speaking words of life to each other, showing up for each other. Again.

But this back and forth is not only directed toward one another. In antiphon, we are talking to God together—praying in agreement, even in the very same words. As Rev. Canon Mary Maggard Hays explains, "We aren't just conversing with each other when we recite the Psalms antiphonally or responsively. We are talking to God, too. Reminding one another and God of his promises and our complaints. We are witnessing one another's cries for help and reminding God that we are in this together."[2]

Often the more charismatic and energetic traditions have a time of call and response, when the congregation and the preacher interact with each other, building a sermon together with "Amens" and "Hallelujahs."

Christian friendships are call-and-response friendships. We tell each other over and over, back and forth, the truth of who we are and who God is. Over dinner and on walks, dropping off soup when someone is sick, and in prayer over the phone, we speak the good news to each other. And we become good news to every other.

My best friendships are with people who are willing to get in the muck with me, who see me as I am, and who speak to me of our hope in Christ in the midst of it. These friends' lives become a sermon to me. I don't mean that we give each other pat answers or cheap pep talks—few things are worse than receiving a neat little packaged sermon after we've poured out our fears or embarrassments to someone. Instead, we hold up the experiences of our lives to the Word of truth.

The Psalms that we speak responsively to each other every Sunday don't offer easy answers. They run the gamut from triumphant praise to deepest depression. They let us be as complex as we actually are. Christian friends are like this. They call to us and respond with us when we say "O LORD, our Lord, how majestic is your name!" (Ps 8:1), and when we say, "O LORD, why do you cast my soul away? Why do you hide your face from me?" (Ps 88:14).

My friendship with Rebekka has become, quite literally, a friendship of call and response.

We call. We leave messages.

We call back.

We respond.

This call and response is the rhythm of good friendship, of life together, of the community of saints.

◆ ◆ ◆

For a couple of centuries now, evangelicals have focused almost exclusively on a personal relationship with God, on individual conversion and spiritual growth. Many feel that the church (if it's necessary at all) is primarily intended to serve our individual spiritual needs or to group us together with like-minded people—a kind of holy fraternity.

If we believe that church is merely a voluntary society of people with shared values, then it is entirely optional. If the church helps you with your personal relationship with God, great; if not, I know a great brunch place that's open on Sunday.

But while an individual relationship with Jesus is an important part of the Christian life, it is not the sum total of the Christian life. Our relationship with God is never less than an intimate relationship with Christ, but it is always more than that. Christians throughout history—Protestants, Catholics, and Orthodox alike—have confessed that it is impossible to have a relationship with Christ outside of a vital relationship with the church, Christ's body and bride. In his *Institutes,* John Calvin quotes Cyprian's famous dictum (drawing on Paul's language in Galatians 4) that "He can no longer have God for his Father, who has not the Church for his mother."[3]

When we confess in the Nicene Creed that we believe in "one holy, catholic, apostolic church," we are confessing that we cannot know Christ on our own, or merely with a small cadre of our friends. Instead, we rely on the global, historic church that Christ initiated and built. When we worship Jesus, we rely on millions of Christians over thousands of years whom God has used to bear witness to himself. The only reason we know anything at all about Jesus is because his disciples told their friends, neighbors, and enemies about him, the apostles preached and wrote down his teaching and stories about him, and believers have carried his message everywhere they've gone in each generation. The Bible names this process *paradosis*—the faithful handing down of the gospel, a process that is always embodied and that happens in real time with real people (1 Cor 11:2; 2 Thess 2:15).

My relationship with Rebekka is not merely relational: two friends who love God and each other. It is institutional, and it is wrapped in ritual. We are both baptized. We are co-communicants. For five years Rebekka and I took communion together each Sunday.

We have a relationship of "call and response" with all believers the world over and throughout time. Beautifully and mysteriously, the community Rebekka and I share is not simply with each other. It is with all of the church.

We are in this together.

Thomas, the priest at the church Rebekka and I used to attend together, often asked us to imagine the communion table stretching on for miles, to remind us that when we take Communion, we mysteriously feast with all those who are in Christ.[4] In the Eucharist we commune with Dorothy Day and Saint Augustine, the apostle Paul and Billy Graham, Flannery O'Connor and my own grandmother. One day we will all feast together, in the flesh, with Christ himself.

Hopefully Rebekka and I will be seated near each other, and near the butter.

◆ ◆ ◆

We profoundly need each other. We are immersed in the Christian life together. There is no merely private faith—everything we are and do as individuals affects the church community.

Yet many believers of my generation are not sure what the church is for. Some have denigrated the need for it all together. We have produced a me-centered faith that would be foreign to most Christians throughout history. We have made a false gospel with individualized communion-on-the-go kits. A popular Christian author can write that "most of the influential Christian leaders I know (who are not pastors) do not attend church," and can refer to the church as a university that he has "graduated" from.[5]

But if Christianity is not only about my individual connection with God, but is instead about God calling, forming, saving, and redeeming a people, then the church can never be relegated to "elective" status. Christ did not send his Holy Spirit only to individuals. He did not merely seek personal relationships with his followers. The good news is not simply that I can believe and thus make it to heaven, or even that I can believe and live out my life among a band of Christian friends.

Jesus sent his Spirit to a people. The preservation of our faith and the endurance of the saints is not an individual promise; it is a promise that God will redeem and preserve his church—a people, a community, an organism, an institution—generation after generation, and that even the gates of hell will not prevail against it.

Michael Ramsey, Archbishop of Canterbury in the mid-twentieth century, wrote, "We do not know the whole fact of Christ incarnate unless we know his church, and its life as part of his own life. . . . The Body is the fullness of Christ, and the history of the Church and the lives of the saints are acts in the biography of the Messiah."[6] We do not know this Messiah solely through the red letters in the gospel texts. We know him in his fullness because we are joined to him in his Body, the church. In this joining, we do not lose our individuality or our individual stories of conversion and encounter with Christ. Instead, our own small stories are wrapped up in the story of all believers throughout time, which are together part of the eternal story of Christ.

◆ ◆ ◆

Yet Christ's bride and body, which will one day be spotless and whole, is currently blemished and broken.

There is, of course, the plain fact of institutional disunity in the church. I have another "friend of my right hand," Faith. She was in my wedding, and I was in hers. Faith is Catholic and, though we love and respect each other deeply, we do not commune together. In our friendship we bear and mourn the fractures in Christ's body.

And beyond the grim reality of institutional disunity, many of us bear scars from fractured relationships or institutional sin in the church.

Rebekka and I have encountered brokenness in our friendship. We've hurt each other. We've had to have long, hard talks. She's been gracious enough to be willing to have them. We've forgiven each other.

There are times, though, when the wounds the church gives are even more profound and complex than conflicts between individuals, as painful as they can be. Sin in the church can be insidious and systemic. We can be injured by a misuse of power or entrenched institutional pathology. Any of us who have hung around the church long enough have a few scars to show.

I was once deeply wounded by someone in a position of power in my church. Suddenly, a place that had always been a refuge for me became a place of rejection and condemnation. The pain of that hurt felt sharp, even physical, a blow that knocked the breath out of me. I was tempted to give up on the church altogether. I felt that everywhere I looked, left and right, I saw ecclesial dysfunction and brokenness. I was becoming cynical and guarded.

Yet where else could I go? The church was where I heard the gospel in community, where I received nourishment in Word and sacrament, where I touched the body of Christ, where I was shaped and formed as one beloved by God. So we returned to church, albeit a different congregation, after a lot of prayer and talks with close friends and mentors. Our new pastor, who knew our story and struggle, called us "the walking wounded." I received the Word and sacrament, most often with tears, among people I was no longer sure I could trust. Yet believers around us loved us and prayed for us. The church itself nursed us slowly and patiently back to health. Brothers and sisters, our co-communicants, met us in our pain, spoke words of life and hope over us, and dared us to trust again.

Many have suffered far worse than me at the hands of the church. The church throughout history has been the world's leader in showing compassion for the poor, suffering, and rejected. It has brought us wonders of architecture, modern medicine, art, and higher education. Yet the church has also been a place of scandal and violence—child abuse, religious wars, racism, and bigotry—all manner of evil. Flannery O'Connor said, "You have to suffer as much from the church as for it. . . . The only thing that makes the church endurable is that somehow it is the body of Christ, and on this we are fed."[7]

I take hope in what the church will one day become—that we, despite our sin, failure, and pain, will one day be made beautiful and new. Yet our task is not simply to dwell on what the church will one day be, but to face what she currently is squarely and honestly, and to seek Christ in and through the body of Christ. Ramsey challenges us:

> Before Christians can say things about what the church ought to be, their first need is to say what the Church is, here and now amid its own failures and the questionings of the bewildered. Looking at it now, with its inconsistencies and perversions and its want of perfection, we must ask what is the real meaning of it just as it is. As the eye gazes upon it, it sees the Passion of Jesus Christ; but the eye of faith sees further: it sees the power of Almighty God.[8]

In the sin and failure of the church, we see the darkness and ugliness for which Christ suffered and died. But we also see the spectacular hope that in the midst of sinners, God can bring forth redemption, repentance, and transformation. We gaze in weakness, with dim eyes, on the power of God.

And here's a further complication: the church is not an entity outside of me. I do not stand on the outside looking in. I am as much part of the church as (in the words of Paul) a hand is a part of a body. That means that when I see sin in the church, I am implicated in it. I contribute to the brokenness of the church. I have dealt wounds to others; I have been unfaithful to the bridegroom. Every church leader and church member is, in no insignificant way, a failure. But here too we see God's power because, in this body of Christ, we find a place where we can be gloriously and devastatingly human. We find a place where we can fail and repent and grow and receive grace and be made new. Like a family—but even closer than a family—we can learn to live together, weak and human, in the goodness and transformation of God.

In the Christian faith it's almost a philosophical principle that the universal is known through the particular and the abstract through the concrete. We love people universally by loving the particular people we know and can name. We love the world by loving a particular place in it—a specific creek or hill or city or block. The incarnation of Jesus is the ultimate example of this principle, when the one who "fills all in all" became a singular baby in a tangible body in a particular place in time.

It's easy for the church to exist only in our mind as an abstract ideal. I can speak of church matters—of ecclesiology—on a cosmic scale, in academic or exalted tones, conjuring vague images of saints in white robes. But our love for the church universal is worked out in the hard pews (or folding chairs) of our particular, local congregation. A local congregation, a parish, is our small, concrete entry into the universal church. It is the basic unit of Christian community and the place where we encounter God in Word and sacrament. The body of Christ—ancient, global, catholic—is only known, loved, and served through the gritty reality of our local context.

And that's where things get both more difficult and more interesting. Because people like Rebekka sit near me in church—people who know me, who get me, who I trust and laugh with as we gather in small group over the study of Scripture and a plate of spaghetti. But there are other people around me in the pews, people I find irritating or awkward, people who vehemently hold political opinions

I find suspect, people with whom I have nothing in common outside of our shared membership in this community of the saints. Some of those I practice call and response with each week would not be people I'd ever want to go with on a long road trip.

The body of Christ is made of all kinds of people, some of whom I find obnoxious, arrogant, self-righteous, or misguided (charges, I'm sure, others have rightly applied to me).

> **Those who were winning at life saw no need for this life-disrupting Savior. The people of God are the losers, misfits, and broken.**

From the beginning, relationships in the church were fraught. Peter and Paul must have made for awkward dinner guests when Paul publically opposed Peter to his face, as we're told in Galatians. If I had been there, I'd likely have changed the subject, offered everyone dessert, and made a note not to invite Peter and Paul to the same party.

We are drawn to those we find lovely and likable. Yet those Jesus spent his time among—and those most drawn to Jesus—were the odd, the disheveled, and the outcast. Those who were winning at life saw no need for this life-disrupting Savior. The people of God are the losers, misfits, and broken. This is good news—and humiliating.

God loves and delights in the people in the pews around me and dares me to find beauty in them. To love his people on earth is to see Christ in them, to live among them, to receive together Word and sacrament. I have stories of meeting fellow parishioners who, at first, I think I could never like but who, over time, become dear to my heart. There's an elderly man I went to church with years ago, a widower with slicked-back hair, polished shoes, and a subtle smell of cigarette smoke and Bengay. The first time we met he said something offensive and seemed crotchety. But we kept showing up to church, and over time I saw how he served those around him and heard more of his story. He walked with a limp and had chronic pain. I began to notice how he'd grin when he saw a toddler dancing in the back of the church. I grew to like him—maybe even, at times, to love him. He limped each week down the aisle to communion—a broken old man, rough around the edges, sometimes mean. And yet he was on his way, limping to redemption.

We work out our faith with these other broken men and women around us in the pews. It's lackluster. It can be boring or taxing. It's often messy. It's sometimes painful. But these Christians around me become each other's call and response. We remind each other of the good news. All saints and sinners in the church share together in this gospel. The meal would be incomplete if even one of these was not at the table. It would not be good news if even one of these members were missing. As Lesslie Newbigin put it, "None of us can be made whole till we are made whole together."[9] If we are saved at all, we are saved together.

—◆◆◆—

To be clear, Rebekka and I are not the church by ourselves. Nor are our relationships with close friends a stand-in for the church. The church is an eternal body, an international organism, an institution made of every tribe, tongue, and nation (Rev 7:9). But we enter that giant reality of Christ's church through the small realities of our week—as I show up at my church in South Austin, take communion, get to know those around me, meet a new visitor, join Christian friends for coffee, and live life among my brothers and sisters.

If ever Rebekka and I love each other well or pray for each other, our friendship is part of the work and mission of the broader organism of Christ's body. When we celebrate my kids' baptisms (Rebekka made cupcakes) or show up for small group Bible study, when we confess to each other, share a meal, or take the Eucharist together, we participate in the life of an international and ancient Christian community—we belong to each other and to those on the other side of the globe.

And today, in my spare minutes, calling a friend on a Tuesday evening, I am part of a larger story—not only the larger story of my friendship with Rebekka but the cosmic story of Christ redeeming his bride. Rebekka and I talk through struggles in our marriages, decisions we're worried about, or a good book we've read, and in this small call and response, we live life together as those baptized, those in the church, those who belong to Christ and, in Christ, to each other.

10

drinking tea

sanctuary and savoring

For the time being, I'm ignoring the toys and socks strewn across my living room to sit on my couch and drink tea. I pause to notice and to savor the dark tea rippling against the bright white of my favorite mug, the twisted branches of late-winter trees outside the window, the warmth of the steam against my face, the dwindling light stretched in long rectangles across the floor.

In our house, quiet moments like this are rare. In order to embrace them, tasks, distractions, and pestering worries have to be willfully set aside.

After God finishes each creative work in Genesis 1, he declares his creation "good" and lavishly gives us free reign to enjoy its goodness. It is no accident that the psalmist enjoins us to taste and see that the Lord is good—not simply to reason or confess that God is good, but to taste it. My body, this tea, and the quiet twilight are teaching me God's goodness through my senses. I'm tasting, hearing, feeling, seeing, and smelling that God is good.

Pleasure is our deep human response to an encounter with beauty and goodness. In these moments of pleasure—of delight, enjoyment, awe, and revelry—we respond to God impulsively with our very bodies: "Yes, we agree! Your creation is very good."

◆ ◆ ◆

I love hot tea. Also coffee, especially iced in the summertime. And baths with a good book. And rainstorms on tin roofs. And homemade guacamole. I love to take walks in the evening, just before the sun sets, when it's quiet. I watch the scenery change with the seasons. My thoughts dart from some big life question to a cat in a window to a hard conversation from the week before to the color of a neighbor's house. Sometimes, during the best walks, I don't notice what I'm thinking about. I just walk, and come home quieted.

Jonathan unwinds with music, sometimes Haydn and other times eighties DC hardcore, both of which hold their own kind of beauty and pleasure. He and I both like to watch TV or a movie together on Friday nights. He prefers apocalyptic shows about zombies killing everyone and I like watching gorgeous people talk to each another, but we make it work.

Mysteriously and wondrously, God revels even more than we do in the slight bitterness of tea, the feel of sunshine on skin, a ripe avocado, a perfect guitar lick, or a good plot twist. In *The Screwtape Letters*, the senior demon Screwtape scolds his underling for allowing his patient the smallest experience of pleasure—a walk in a beautiful place, tea, or a good book which he read "because he enjoyed it and not in order to make clever remarks about it to his friends." Both pleasure and pain, says Screwtape, are "unmistakably real, and therefore . . . they give the man who feels them a touchstone of reality."[1] He diabolically warns that people should not be allowed to maintain any "personal taste . . . even if it is something quite trivial such as a fondness for country cricket or collecting stamps or drinking cocoa." Though small practices of enjoyment may seem trivial, the demon sees in them "a sort of innocence and humility and self-forgetfulness."[2]

＊ ＊ ＊

Our culture's relationship with pleasure is complex. On one hand, we seem obsessed with pleasure. We overindulge and overeat. We are addicted to amusement and are overwhelmed by pornography, sexual gratuity, and violence, both on screens and off. Ironically, greed and consumerism dull our delight. The more we indulge, the less pleasure we find. We are hedonistic cynics and gluttonous stoics. In our consumerist society we spend endless energy and money seeking pleasure, but we are never sated.

Pragmatism, another powerful cultural force, can denigrate our desire for beauty and enjoyment—we don't build parking decks for their aesthetic appeal, we just need somewhere to put our cars. Workaholism and constant connectivity fight against our ability to be present to the pleasure of the moment.

The church has a reputation for being antipleasure. Many characterize Christians in general the way H. L. Mencken wryly described Puritans: people with a "haunting fear that someone, somewhere might be happy."[3]

In reality, the church has led the way in the art of enjoyment and pleasure. New Testament scholar Ben Witherington points out that it was the church, not Starbucks, that created coffee culture.[4] Coffee was first invented by Ethiopian monks—the term *cappuccino* refers to the shade of brown used for the habits of the Capuchin monks of Italy. Coffee is born of extravagance, an extravagant God who formed an extravagant people, who formed a craft out of the pleasures of roasted beans and frothed milk.

—◆◆◆—

A culture formed by the gospel will honor good and right enjoyment, celebration, and sensuousness. Christian worship and community have left a legacy of beauty: the paintings of Rembrandt, the poems of Gerard Manley Hopkins, the music of Bach and U2, basilicas, iconography, King cakes, Guinness, craft-brewed beer; the list could go on and on. Even the Puritans, derided by Mencken, seem like paragons of pleasure compared to overworked, stressed-out modern Americans. Puritan communities set aside a day every month for community recreation. It was a day for play and leisure, a big city-wide party.[5] Despite the stereotype, Puritans were also big proponents of celebrating the pleasures of marital sex, even for women.[6]

**Coffee is born of extravagance, an extravagant
God who formed an extravagant people,
who formed a craft out of the pleasures
of roasted beans and frothed milk.**

When we enjoy God's creation, we reflect God himself. God does not stoically pronounce creation "good," like a disinterested manager checking off a quality checklist so he can clock out early. God delights in the perfect acoustics of ocean waves, swoons over the subtle intensity of dark chocolate, and glories in robins' eggs and peacock calls.

G. K. Chesterton saw in God a childlike wonder. Children never tire of beauty and pleasure. They embrace enjoyment with abandon. They don't feel guilty about taking time to search for feathers, invent a game, or enjoy a treat. Chesterton imagines that God revels in the pleasure of his creation like an enthusiastic child:

> Because children have abounding vitality, because they are in spirit fierce and free, therefore they want things repeated and unchanged. They always say, "Do it again"; and the grown-up person does it again until he is nearly dead. For grown-up people are not strong enough to exult in monotony. But perhaps God is strong enough to exult in monotony. It is possible that God says every morning, "Do it again" to the sun; and every evening, "Do it again" to the moon. It may not be automatic necessity that makes all daisies alike; it may be that God makes every daisy separately, but has never got tired of making them. It may be that He has the eternal appetite of infancy; for we have sinned and grown old, and our Father is younger than we.[7]

We have sinned and grown old, and become dulled to the wonders around us. Though it may seem counterintuitive, enjoyment takes practice. Throughout our life we must relearn the abandon of revelry and merriment.

Throughout Christian history, Christian worship has been a profoundly sensuous experience, a training ground for pleasure and delight.

Christians are singing people. From ancient monks chanting the Psalms to Wesleyan hymnody, music has always been a way for the church to hone its theology and practice prayer with artistry and beauty. On every Sunday in every corner of the earth you can find Christians singing. From Gregorian chant to African-American spirituals to acoustic worship bands to Syriac chant to East African kwaya, we hear music echoing from every gathered community of Christians.[8]

At its best, church architecture accents the beauty of light and shadow, space and shape. This doesn't mean that every sanctuary looks the same. I've worshiped in a school cafeteria, a thatched-roof hut, a stone cathedral with soaring ceilings, and a tiny country church, and in each place the worshipers thoughtfully sought to make their space beautiful, knowing that God is worthy to be worshiped in and through beauty.

Peek into a worship space and you'll find incense, flowers, bright whites of vestments, dancing, candles, banners, or works of art and music. Glory. We taste, we smell, we hear, we see, we feel. Our senses come alive in worship.

At my church, before anyone speaks a word, the sanctuary already whispers a story. We see a parade of colors changing with the seasons: purple, then white, then green, sometimes red. The room is filled with candles—the gospel and epistle candles are always lit together, symbolizing the unity of the Scriptures, and a tall white candle, called the Christ candle, towers in the center. There are seasons when the sanctuary is decorated and ornate and seasons when it is stripped and plain. There's a font filled with water and a table draped in linens. There's a chalice and a plate.

These symbols and aesthetics silently retell the story of Christ's life and teach theology. For most of history the majority of believers could not read, so Christian worship intentionally taught the gospel in preliterate ways. But even now, each of us, whether first graders or physics professors, still learn the gospel in preliterate ways. We absorb it. We learn what we believe, as James K. A. Smith says, from our "body up."[9] We have to taste and see that God is good if we are ever going to really believe it.

Christian worship trains us to recognize and respond to beauty. We learn to embrace the pleasures of being human and of human culture. Our God-given, innate thirst for enjoyment and sensuousness is directed toward the one who alone can quench it, the God who we were made to enjoy forever.

This looks different from culture to culture. In a remote East African church, I lifted the chalice to my lips and was surprised that instead of wine, I tasted Coca-Cola. Wine was hard to come by where we were, and grape juice was nonexistent. Coke was the beverage of extravagance. A missionary told me that on Christmas morning children got two treats: meat and Coca-Cola. Coke was used in worship because these believers wanted to use the finest and the best. And indeed, that Sunday, it was an indulgent pleasure. Christ was among us, and even in the midst of poverty, worship was lavish.

The room where we worship is called a sanctuary, from the Latin *sanctuarium*, a derivative of *sanctus*, or "holy." The word *sanctuary* refers to a holy place but, because churches were once places of legal asylum, the term has also come to mean a place of shelter, a haven, or a refuge.

In my daily life I find moments of sanctuary, moments when wonder scoots up next to me with a nudge. I remember how well I'm provided for. This quiet moment with my cup of tea is a moment of sanctuary in every sense—a haven of beauty and a place of worship. The steam warms my face like incense.

◆ ◆ ◆

In *Letters to Malcolm,* C. S. Lewis devotes a delightful letter to the subject of pleasure. His advice: begin where you are. He writes that he once thought he had to start "by summoning up what we believe about the goodness and greatness of God, by thinking about creation and redemption and 'all the blessings of this life.'"[10] Instead, he says, we ought to begin with the pleasures at hand—for him, a walk beside a babbling brook; for me at the moment, the wonder of hot water and dried leaves.

Most of us love these moments in our day at a gut level. We intuitively know that goodness and beauty are connected to the divine, that "every good and perfect gift is from above, coming down from the Father of lights" (Jas 1:17). We aren't overly ascetic fundamentalists trying to stamp out delight or pleasure wherever it is found. We naturally greet these moments with gratitude. But more than that, we respond with adoration. We are not only grateful for pleasure; our hearts wonder what kind of Creator makes a world that overflows with such loveliness and beauty. As Lewis says, "One's mind runs back up the sunbeam to the sun."[11]

Yet so much wars against these little moments of glory in our day. For me, anxiety and needling worries are always clanging in the background, robbing me of the ability to simply exhale. I have to learn to surrender, to give up my flimsy illusion of control, and relax into beauty.

As busy, practical, hurried, and distracted people, we develop habits of inattention and miss these tiny theophanies in our day. But if we were fully alive and whole, no pleasure would be too ordinary or commonplace to stir up adoration.[12]

I have to learn the habits of adoration intentionally—to get out of my head and stop to notice the colors in my daughter's eyes or the sound of rain on our back porch. Part of me—the Taskmaster General in my brain—can feel guilty about the moments when I slow down to enjoy the beauty around me. Tea and an empty hour can feel frivolous or frittering. I feel guilty about not doing something more important with my time, like laundry or balancing the checkbook or meeting my neighbors or working or volunteering or serving the poor.

Those are, of course, important things to do and good and necessary ways to use time. But it takes strength to enjoy the world, and we must exercise a kind of muscle to revel and delight. If we neglect exercising that muscle—if we never savor a lazy afternoon, if we must always be cleaning out the fridge or volunteering at church or clocking in more hours—we'll forget how to notice beauty and we'll miss the unmistakable reality of goodness that pleasure trains us to see. We must take up the practice—the privilege and responsibility—of noticing, savoring, reveling, so that, to use Annie Dillard's phrase, "creation need not play to an empty house."[13]

A few years ago, several months after the birth of my first child, I was completely exhausted. It seemed that my life and my body were the property of a tiny, adorable little dictator. It had been a year of transition and, besides new motherhood, there was a lot of upheaval and turmoil in my life.

During this time I met with my wise friend and mentor, Father Kenny. I complained to him that I didn't know what to give up for Lent. I felt overwhelmed. He said to me, "You don't need to give anything up. Your whole life is Lent right now." He told me to take up the practice of pleasure: to intentionally embrace enjoyment as a discipline.[14]

So for Lent that year I walked to my favorite coffee shop once a week and enjoyed a vanilla steamer and a novel. It was a discipline, for sure, in that it took commitment and coordinating childcare and setting aside work, but self-denial it was not.

The rigors of motherhood, ministry, and simply being a grown-up in a broken world had hollowed me out. I was brittle, irritable, undernourished, and overextended. Making space for one hour of pure enjoyment began to fill my hollowness with a weighty kind of joy. I read *The Book of Sorrows* by Walter Wangerin, the perfect Lenten novel.[15] I finished it during the Easter season on a family trip. As I read about the hero, the Dun Cow, nursing a starving, fearful coyote, I found myself on my knees, sobbing. God powerfully comforted me through that scene, speaking to me of his love, provision, and care for me. God met me—wrecked me, really—through that novel in a way that I can only describe as mystical. But I had no idea that would happen when I took up the discipline of pleasure. One of the most intense healing experiences of my life came as a total surprise after I simply made space to enjoy something for the sake of enjoying it.

* * *

Pleasure is a gift, but it can become an idol. We overindulge. We become addicts. What once was a gift becomes a trap. Carolyn Arends explores Lewis's ideas about pleasure in an essay about her love for chile con queso, saying:

> The enjoyment we feel upon receiving a Need-pleasure—water to quench thirst, for example, or the scratching of an itch—is intense but short-lived. But with Appreciation-pleasures—nonessential things that awaken us to delight, like delicious smells and tastes and scenes of beauty—the sensation intensifies over time. Greed—the

repeated cry of "Encore!" to, say, rich black coffee or extra-creamy queso—may transform a Pleasure of Appreciation into a Pleasure of Need, draining out of it all the lasting enjoyment.[16]

The cry of "Encore!"—the demand for more and more and ever more—can turn a healthy pleasure into an addiction. We become insatiable. Our ability to enjoy something is diminished to the extent that it becomes a false god. God alone can be both worshiped and enjoyed. All lesser things are meant to be enjoyed in their proper place, as they flow from the God who deserves all worship. Arends sums up, "The answer, Lewis contends, is not to avoid pleasure but to 'have' and 'read' it properly: to receive it, open-handed, as both a gift and a message."[17]

There is a symbiotic relationship—cross-training, if you will—between the pleasures we find in gathered worship and those in my teacup or in a warm blanket or in the smell of bread baking.

Enjoyment requires discernment. It can be a gift to wrap up in a blanket and lose myself in a TV show, but we can also "amuse ourselves to death."[18] My pleasure in wine or tea or exercise is good in itself but can become disordered. As we learn to practice enjoyment, we need to learn the craft of discernment—how to enjoy rightly, to "have" and "read" pleasure well.

There is a symbiotic relationship—cross-training, if you will— between the pleasures we find in gathered worship and those in my teacup or in a warm blanket or in the smell of bread baking. Lewis reminds us that "one must walk before one can run. . . . [We] shall not be able to adore God on the highest occasions if we have learned no habit of doing so on the lowest. At best, our faith and reason will tell us that he is adorable but we shall not have *found* him so."[19]

These tiny moments of beauty in our days train us in the habits of adoration and discernment. And the pleasure and sensuousness of our gathered worship teach us to look for and receive these small moments in our days. Together, they train us in the art of noticing and of reveling in God's goodness and artistry.

A few weeks ago, I was walking to work, standing on the corner by the Tire and Auto Parts store, waiting to cross the street, when I suddenly heard church bells begin to ring, loud and long. I froze, riveted. They were beautiful, a moment of transcendence right in the middle of the grimy street. Glory next to the Discount Tire and Auto Parts.

Liturgical worship has been referred to, sometimes derisively, as "smells and bells" because of the sensuous way Christians have historically worshiped. Smells—the sweet and pungent smell of incense—and bells—like the ones I heard in my neighborhood, which rang out from a Catholic church.

At my church we ring bells during our practice of the Eucharist. The acolyte (the person—often a child—assisting the priest) rings chimes when our pastor prepares the communion meal. There is nothing magic about these chimes; nothing superstitious. They are just bells. We ring them in the Eucharistic liturgy, as a way of saying, "Pay attention." They are an alarm to rouse the congregation, to jostle us to attention, telling us to take note, sit up, lean forward, and notice Christ in our midst. We need this kind of embodied beauty—smells and bells—in our gathered worship, and we need it in our ordinary day to remind us to take notice of Christ right where we are.

Dostoyevsky wrote that "beauty will save the world."[20] This might strike us as mere hyperbole. But as our culture increasingly rejects the idea and language of truth, the church's role as a harbinger of beauty is a powerful witness to the God of all beauty. Czesław Miłosz wrote in his poem "One More Day":

Though the good is weak, beauty is very strong . . .
And when people cease to believe that there is good and evil
Only beauty will call to them and save them
So that they still know how to say: this is true and that is false.[21]

Being curators of beauty, pleasure, and delight is therefore an intrinsic part of our mission, a mission that recognizes the reality that truth is beautiful.

These moments of loveliness—good tea, bare trees, and soft shadows—are church bells. In my dimness, they jolt me to attention, and remind me that Christ is in our midst. His song of truth, sung by his people all over the world, echoes down my ordinary street, spilling even into my living room.

11

sleeping

sabbath, rest, and the work of God

A comprehensive study in the United Kingdom recently revealed that kids learn to rest in the same way they learn to walk, run, and talk.[1] Rest takes practice.

We need a ritual and routine to learn to fall asleep. Infants learn by habit, over time, how to cease fighting sleepiness. A regular bedtime, dim lights, bath time, book time, rocking, allow their brains to carve out a pattern, a biochemical path to rest. Without a ritual and routine, they become hyperactive and often exhibit behavioral problems. Adults aren't much different. I'm certainly not.

If rest is learned through habit and repetition, so is restlessness. These habits of rest or restlessness form us over time.

There is a profound connection between the sleep we get in our beds each night and the sacramental rest we know each Sunday in our gathered worship. Both gathered worship and our sleep habits profess our loves, our trusts, and our limits. Both involve discipline and ritual. Both require that we cease relying on our own effort and activity and lean on God for his sufficiency. Both expose our vulnerability. Both restore.

The liturgy of my night—lock the doors, brush my teeth, get a glass of water, turn out the lights, pull back the covers, crawl into bed, curl up, close my eyes—is a repetitive, mundane, and good thing, through which I've learned to slow down, to let go of the day behind me, and go to sleep. Similarly, corporate worship trains us, over time, to cease striving to make our own way and our own righteousness and to receive God's means of grace.

◆ ◆ ◆

Our sleep habits both reveal and shape our loves. A decent indicator of what we love is that for which we willingly give up sleep. I love my kids, so I sacrifice sleep for them (often)—I nurse our baby or comfort our eldest after a nightmare. I love my husband and my close friends so I stay up late to keep a good conversation going a bit longer. Or I rise early to pray or to take a friend to the airport.

But my willingness to sacrifice sleep also reveals less noble loves. I stay up later than I should, drowsy, collapsed on the couch, vaguely surfing the Internet, watching cute puppy videos. Or I stay up trying to squeeze more activity into the day, to pack it with as much productivity as possible. My disordered sleep reveals a disordered love, idols of entertainment or productivity.

My willingness to sacrifice much-needed rest and my prioritizing amusement or work over the basic needs of my body and the people around me (with whom I'm far more likely to be short-tempered after a night of little sleep) reveal that these good things—entertainment and work—have taken a place of ascendancy in my life. In the nitty-gritty of my daily life, repentance for idolatry may look as pedestrian as shutting off my email an hour earlier or resisting that alluring clickbait to go to bed.

The truth is, I'm far more likely to give up sleep for entertainment than I am for prayer. When I turn on Hulu late at night I don't consciously think, "I value this episode of *Parks and Rec* more than my family, prayer, and my own body." But my habits reveal and shape what I love and what I value, whether I care to admit it or not.

> **In the nitty-gritty of my daily life, repentance for idolatry may look as pedestrian as shutting off my email an hour earlier or resisting that alluring clickbait to go to bed.**

Sleep habits also reveal and shape what we trust. We lie awake fretting about our job or our health or the people we love. The wee hours greet us with our problems and our inability to solve them. What we trust in, lying in our beds at the end of a long day, is where our hearts truly lie.

The psalmist declares, "Unless the LORD watches over the city, the watchman stays awake in vain. It is in vain that you rise up early and go late to rest, eating the bread of anxious toil; for he gives to his beloved sleep" (Ps 127:1-2). It is God who watches over our city and who ultimately determines our safety. God has called us his beloved and he is faithful to provide for and protect his people, so we can savor his good gift of rest.

In the *Book of Common Prayer*, Anglicans have four short times of daily prayer—morning, noon, evening (known as Vespers), and night. Of the four, my favorite is the night service, called Compline. The prayers are soothing and comforting. They seem to invite whispering. "Guide us waking, O Lord, and guard us sleeping; that awake we may watch with Christ, and asleep we may rest in peace."[2]

Guard us and guide us, we pray.

In our nighttime prayers we remember the drama night holds, the stark vulnerability that we face from dusk till dawn: "Keep watch, dear Lord, with those who work, or watch, or weep this night, and give your angels charge over those who sleep. Tend the sick, Lord Christ; give rest to the weary, bless the dying, soothe the suffering, pity the afflicted, shield the joyous; and all for your love's sake. Amen."[3]

Our need for sleep reveals that we have limits. We are unable to defend ourselves, to keep ourselves safe, to master the world around us. Sleep exposes reality. We are frail and weak. We need a guide and a guard.

No matter how much I love or fear something, ultimately my human need for rest kicks in. Even when my kids are sick and really need me, I can't stay awake with them day and night for long. Our powerful need for sleep is a reminder that we are finite. God is the only one who never slumbers nor sleeps.

A few years ago a Sprint commercial proclaimed defiantly, "I want—no, I have the right—to be unlimited." This is the message we receive from our culture: no limits. Nothing should stop you, slow you down, or limit your freedom. Not even human embodiment. You can be unlimited, and if you're not, someone's to blame. We believe that we need better technology, better efficiency, and better organization so that we can exist as people unbridled from creaturely limits. We can be boundless, competent, and utterly self-determining.

According to data from the National Health Interview Survey, nearly 30 percent of adults average less than six hours of sleep per night, significantly under the recommended seven to eight hours. Only about 30 percent of high school students reported getting at least eight hours of sleep on an average school night, though they need around ten. In one national study, over 7 percent of people between twenty-five and thirty-five admitted to actually nodding off while driving in the past month. In 2013 the Centers for Disease Control and Prevention declared, "Insufficient Sleep Is a Public Health Problem."[4]

Most of us have heard statistics like this before. And we yawn and pour more coffee. We know, we know. We're busy, we're tired, we're worn out.

But this public health epidemic is indicative of a spiritual crisis—a culture of disordered love and disordered worship. We disdain limits. Wendell Berry warned, "It is easy . . . to imagine that the next great division of the world will be between people who wish to live as creatures and people who wish to live as machines."[5]

The holiness of rest and the blessedness of unproductivity is a foreign idea to many of us. We're people of twenty-four-hour big-box stores, wee hour drive-throughs, and all-night coffee shops. We have late night TV and late, late night TV. We have five-hour energy shots available in the grocery store check-out line.

Granted, some of us are sleepless because of a physical disorder, and I'm grateful for treatments that help combat medical insomnia. Some, as a prayer in Compline reminds us, "work while others sleep,"[6] and we need these people (nurses, doctors, midwives, firefighters, police officers, guards, and so many others) who sacrifice sleep to serve those around them.

But many of us resist sleep for other reasons. We've developed routines of restlessness in our daily lives. We are out of step with the reality of our needs and limits. Rod Dreher explains how we rebel against our finitude: "Without recognizing that there are limits written into nature by nature's God, there is nothing to keep humankind from transgressing nature, including human nature, to reshape it in our image."[7]

Our bodily limits are our chief daily reminder that we are but dust. We inhabit a frail, vulnerable humanity. And we hate being reminded.

◆ ◆ ◆

Our need for sleep reminds us of our ultimate limit: we are going to die. In an episode of the radio show *This American Life*, Ira Glass admits that his fear of sleeping goes "hand in hand with the fear of death . . . a small taste of the big sleep."[8] One man Glass interviews says that when he goes through his day—driving to work, stuck in traffic, busy with friends and family—he doesn't think about his mortality, but that lying in bed half-asleep he remembers, to his horror, that he will die. Glass interviews others who wake up afraid, unable to fall back asleep, remembering with terror that their death is fast approaching.

Christian spirituality calls us, in the words of Saint Benedict, to keep "the prospect of death before your eyes every day."[9] Each Ash Wednesday we remember together that we are dust, and to dust we shall return.[10] This practice isn't meant to be morbid. Most of us spend much time and energy trying to avoid the reality that we and those we love will die. But in facing the reality of death, we learn how to live rightly. We learn how to live in light of our limits and the brevity of our lives. And we learn to live in the hope of the resurrection.

Sleep serves as a daily memento mori, a reminder of our death. In the Scriptures, the terms death and sleep are often used interchangeably. When we go to sleep each night, we say with the psalmist, "I lie down and sleep; I wake again, because the LORD sustains me" (Ps 3:5 NIV). And we proclaim with the church, "We lay down in death; we wake again because the Lord is risen indeed." In our vulnerable nights we recall our ultimate vulnerability. But in recalling our frailty we get to practice, in the gentlest of ways, relying on God's mercy and care for us.

By embracing sleep each day we submit to the humiliation of our creatureliness and fragility. And in that place of weakness we learn to rest in the reality that our life and death—our days and everything in them—are hidden in Christ.

◆ ◆ ◆

Resisting limits isn't new for the human race. From the very beginning we've had an animosity toward finitude and boundaries. In their rebellion, Adam and Eve wanted to be "like God." Invincible. All-sufficient. Autonomous. Limitless.

But every evening, whether we like it or not, we must admit again that we are not unlimited. Our bodies get tired. Our efforts prove futile. We are needy. Yielding to sleep confesses this reality: a confession that is countercultural and revolutionary. We are not sufficient; we need a caretaker. And this must affect our bodily routines, our worship, and our view of God.

Our culture of restlessness and limitlessness has not only affected our bodies. It has shaped our faith. As Americans and as evangelicals, the subtle idea that our relationship with God relies on our own efforts and energy is part of our DNA. The idea that our bodies don't matter and that limits are simply obstacles to be overcome misshapes our understanding of worship and mission.

Mark Galli has said, "The strength of the evangelical movement is its activism; the weakness of the evangelical movement is its activism."[11] Evangelicalism's energetic history has produced genuine and needed changes in society: the progress of women's rights, the protection of children, and antislavery legislation, among many others. But it can also foster attitudes that deprecate sustainability and rest. When our zealous activism is coupled with a culture of frenzy and grandiosity, the aim of our Christian life can become a list of goals, initiatives, meetings, conferences, and activities that leave us exhausted.

Wesleyan ministers in early evangelicalism—often called "circuit riders"—were expected to work between ninety and one hundred hours a week. So many early ministers collapsed under sheer exhaustion that the church created a "worn-out ministers' fund."[12] Note that the rash of worn-out ministers did not cause the movement to rethink its tactics. It did not generate a theological discussion around the ideas of rest and the sustainable Christian life. Instead, they started a fund—another activist cause to rally around.

Worn-out ministers are part of our evangelical heritage. They're our predecessors and our heroes. And many of us continue in that legacy. We are worn-out ministers, worn-out parents, worn-out business people, worn-out believers.

This affects our worship together. We are prone to embrace a faith that is full of adrenaline, excitement, and activity. But we have to learn together to approach a Savior who invites the weary to come to him for rest.

◀ ◆ ▶

Soon after we were married, Jonathan and I took up the ancient practice of Sabbath-keeping or observing the Lord's Day each Sunday. We were grad students at the time, so giving up our study hours on Sunday afternoons was a huge shift in schedule for us. But we began a routine—which has now spanned over a decade—of beginning Sunday by going to church and then coming home to nap, to savor a long walk, and to have a slow night of pleasure-reading or just hanging out together.

It took me years to realize that our time of gathered worship on Sunday morning and our Sunday afternoon naps are interrelated. Rest is not simply a physical need—it is not only our brains and muscles and eyelids that must learn habits of rest. We need holistic rest—physical, psychological, and spiritual. Worship and bodily rest are wrapped up together. We learn the rhythms of spiritual rest through worship. We learn that we are limited by our sin, our humanity, our moment of history. We need rituals and practices to teach us to receive God's grace and renewal. We need other believers—the church over two thousand years—to help tutor us in Christian wholeness. We must take up the practices of resting in God and in his gifts to us.

In his book *Beyond Smells and Bells*, Mark Galli warns that the achievement culture bred into Western evangelicals affects our worship. Gathered worship can become a place of self-reliance and striving where we seek to achieve a particular spiritual mood or experience by our own effort. Instead, Jesus calls us to give up our faith in our own spiritual striving and to abide in him. "The liturgy is the place where we wait for Jesus to show up. We don't have to do much. The liturgy is not an act of will. It is not a series of activities designed to attain a spiritual or mental state." In worship, we show up, we abide, and we rest. And as Galli says, "If we will dwell there, remain in place, wait patiently, Jesus will show up."[13]

When I first began to attend a church that worshiped with historic liturgy, I cried every week. I hadn't realized it, but for most of my life my worship experience had been marked by my own striving to get to a particular emotional or cognitive place—a place of joy or crisis or emotion or ardent doctrinal affirmation.

But as we stumbled into a small, stone-walled Anglican church one Sunday, I felt too tired and weak to work myself up—my heart or my head—to any emotional climax or intellectual achievement. So I sat in church and followed the script and said my lines.

The words of the liturgy felt like a mother rocking me, singing over me, speaking words of blessing again and again. I was relaxing into the church like an overtired child collapsing on her mom. When my husband and I would get into the car after church each week and talk about the service, I would say to him, "It feels like chamomile tea." This was my weird way of saying that worship allowed me to rest, to relax into the ancient practices and words of the church.

In Jewish culture, days begin in the evening with the setting of the sun. (We see this in Genesis 1 with the repetition of "And there was evening and there was morning.") The day begins with rest. We start by settling down and going to sleep.

This understanding of time is powerfully reorienting, even jarring, to those of us who measure our days by our own efforts and accomplishments. The Jewish day begins in seemingly accomplishing nothing at all. We begin by resting, drooling on our pillow, dropping off into helplessness. Eugene Peterson says, "The Hebrew evening/morning sequence conditions us to the rhythms of grace. We go to sleep and God begins his work."[14]

Though the day begins in darkness, God is still at work, growing crops, healing wounds, giving rest, protecting, guarding, mending, redeeming.[15] We drop out of consciousness, but the Holy Spirit remains at work.

In his brief theology of sleep, Scottish pastor John Baillie writes that in Christ, we "wake up better men than when we went to sleep."[16] If it is hard for us to believe that God is at work in us and in the world even while we sleep, it reveals who we truly think is the mover and maker of our lives and spiritual health. Baillie speaks of God's unlimited, constant activity in the world and in us:

> We habitually suppose ourselves to be more the masters of our spiritual development than we actually are. . . . If some of the processes that are necessary for our physical well-being go on more advantageously in sleep than in waking life, because the will relaxes its too despotic control, why should not the same be true of some of the processes that advance our spiritual well-being?[17]

This is the heart of worship—both our gathered worship on Sundays and worship in our ordinary days. As children beloved and pleasing to God, we join in with what God has already begun. We join in his work in and through his church.

So I cried each week in the worship service. I was learning to rest in a new habit of worship, a way of approaching God that was less reliant on my own energy, effort, or emotional state. I showed up to church like a person drowning, energy spent and arms weakened, and collapsed on the words and practices of the historic church like a life raft.

What if Christians were known as a countercultural community of the well-rested—people who embrace our limits with zest and even joy?

❖ ❖ ❖

We learn to rest by practice, by routine, over time. This is true of our bodies, our minds, and our souls, which are always intertwined.

About one third of our lives are spent in sleep. Through these collective years of rest, God is at work in us and in the world, redeeming, healing, and giving grace. Each night when we yield to sleep, we practice letting go of our reliance on self-effort and abiding in the good grace of our Creator. Thus embracing sleep is not only a confession of our limits; it is also a joyful confession of God's limitless care for us. For Christians, the act of ceasing and relaxing into sleep is an act of reliance on God.

What if Christians were known as a countercultural community of the well-rested—people who embrace our limits with zest and even joy? As believers we can relish sleep as not only necessary but as an embodied response to the truth of Scripture: we are finite, weak creatures who are abundantly cared for by our strong and loving Creator.

In our workaholic, image-barraged, overcaffeinated, entertainment-addicted, and supercharged culture, submission to our creatureliness is a necessary and often overlooked part of discipleship.[18] In my work among graduate students, I encourage students to quit working earlier, take care of their bodies, and get more sleep. It's often the most spiritually helpful and relevant advice I can give. But it doesn't seem like very spiritual advice. It doesn't take a seminary degree to tell someone to get to bed earlier. An enthusiastic report that Christian students are getting longer and deeper sleep likely won't impress many people.

Nevertheless, God cares about sleep. One of my favorite moments in the Gospels is when Jesus conks out in the back of a boat in the middle of a storm. His sleep was theological, in that it displayed an unwavering trust in his Father. But let's not forget that it was also an ordinary example of a tired man taking a nap.

God wants to give us not just lives of holiness and prayer but also of sufficient rest. And perhaps a key step toward a life of prayer and holiness is simply receiving the gift of a good night's sleep.

In Scripture, in the incarnation, and in the church, we learn that grace comes to us through the tangible, earthy world, through the hours of an average day. The gift of rest comes to us through ritual and routine. Unearned and abundant, it comes in repetition, in the learning of a habit, in the liturgy of the day.

At the end of every day, we lie in our beds. Even the most ordinary of days has shaped us—imperceptibly but truly. By a grace we do not control, we yield to sleep. We rest. Our muscles release. Our jaw slacks. We are exposed and weak. We drift out of consciousness. Yet we are still held fast. Our Guard and Guide has called us "beloved," and gives his beloved sleep.

acknowledgments

Thank you to the great team at IVP—especially to Cindy Bunch for not only being a great editor and guide, but also for being the kind of person who I'm better for knowing. Also, thank you to Ethan McCarthy for his patience, hard work, and encouragement throughout the editing process.

Thanks to the leaders and colleagues at the 2014 NISET Writing Workshop, who first made me think that I might have a book in me, and especially to Al Hsu for his wisdom and encouragement (and the writer's license!). Thank you to InterVarsity Christian Fellowship, especially to my friends in GFM South Central and in Women in the Academy and Professions. Thanks also to the leadership students in our grad student chapters at Vanderbilt and the University of Texas, who were my cheerleaders and inspiration along the way.

Thank you to those Facebook and Twitter friends who answered random survey questions about their daily lives, and who have responded to and shared articles and essays I've written. You are a very important part of why I've been able to write.

I am grateful to Andy Crouch for generously offering wisdom and encouragement to me as a new writer, and for his beautiful and kind foreword. I am forever grateful. Thanks also to Rod Dreher for sharing my work and encouraging me to keep writing (and also to his wife, Julie, for her welcome and friendship).

Thank you to Eric and Keri Stumberg, Kevin and DeAnn Stuart, and the whole Stokes family for providing space for me to get away and write.

I cannot express enough love and gratitude to the close friends who have prayed for me and walked with me as I wrote this book. There are more than I could name. But special thanks to the writing prayer team, to Don Paul and Ginger Gross, Alice and Tim Colegrove, Nathan and Leann Barczi, Grace and Cody Spriggs, Rebekka and Manley Seale, Kenny and Katy Hutson, Blake Mathews and Krista Vossler, Steve Dilley and Andrea Palpant Dilley, Sarah Puryear, Steven and Bethany Hebbard, and Woody Giles (aka Uncle Woody). Y'all are good news to me.

Special thanks to Brie Tschoepe and Kelsey Balaban for friendship and helpful feedback on portions of this manuscript.

Thanks to Fr. Kenny Benge and Fr. Thomas McKenzie for being helpful sounding-boards (over plates of Baja Burrito) for the initial ideas in this book, and for encouraging me to write and to be brave in general. I am very grateful to Rev. Canon Mary Maggard Hays for her pastoral care, wisdom, and example. Immense thanks to Fr. Perry and Wendy Koon and Fr. Shawn and Michelle McCain, for being friends and physicians. Thanks also to Shawn and Michelle for giving feedback on portions of drafts of this book.

I am grateful to the pastors and members of Christ the King Cambridge, who let me wrestle out loud with these ideas in ridiculously embryonic form at their winter retreat. Your questions and responses were gracious and helpful. Thanks also to Redeemer

Nashville, for loving and supporting us in so many ways, and to Resurrection South Austin, for being people who help us live (together with you) in the goodness of God.

I'd like to extend enormous gratitude to Marcia Bosscher, who was the first person to think I was a writer and is a constant source of wisdom and strength. She has provided editing, nurture, and light over the years and throughout this project. If ever I've written anything that has helped anyone in any way, Marcia is partially responsible.

Thank you to Sandra and Jerry Dover and all of the Atlanta family for your unshakable love and support. Thank you also to Laura and James Mayes and David and Laci Harrison and their families, for keeping me humble and keeping me laughing. I love y'all.

Becoming a mother has convinced me that I cannot ever adequately thank my parents. They've provided lifelong love and support, from first steps to watching my kids as I wrote the first draft of this book. Thanks to Les and Loraine Harrison, Dad and Mom, for everything. I hope we find ourselves on your back porch soon!

Lastly, thank you to my girls, my geese, my daughters, Flannery and Raine, for being the brightest spots in my day and the twinkliest stars in my sky. This book represents sacrifice on their part and for that, and for them, I am grateful beyond words. And to Jonathan. Not only has he provided friendship, love, and tremendous encouragement as I've written but, as a priest and scholar, he's offered invaluable resources and insight. I am very glad we are in this together.

And glory be to the Word, from whom any goodness in our little words flows, and by whom they will be redeemed.

discussion questions and practices

Here are some questions for reflection, which you can journal about on your own or discuss with a group. There are several practices listed for each chapter. Read through them and try the one that seems best for you. (The expectation is not that you'll complete them all like a task list.) If you are meeting with a group, check in with each other about which practices you tried and how they went.

1. WAKING: BAPTISM AND LEARNING TO BE BELOVED

1. Do you normally wake up quickly or slowly? Chipper or drowsy?

2. In a typical day, what are your first conscious thoughts as you wake up? How do they shape your day and your life?

3. What practices might help you recall in your first waking moments that you are beloved and a part of God's people?

4. Is it hard to believe you are beloved of God? If so, what are some of the obstacles to embracing your identity as beloved?

5. What do you remember about your baptism or what have you been told about it? How has your baptism affected your life and your view of God and the church?

159

6. The author says, "We tend to want a Christian life with the dull bits cut out." Do you struggle with this? If so, how?

7. What do you think the mostly unrecorded "ordinary years" of Jesus' life mean for us? For our understanding of God, worship, and mission?

8. The author quotes Annie Dillard: "How we spend our days is, of course, how we spend our lives." How does this impact the way you think about your days and your Christian life?

Suggested Practices:

1. Each morning, first thing, remember your baptism and belovedness by either crossing yourself, saying aloud "I am clothed in Christ and beloved by God," or another gesture of your own choosing. Notice how this impacts your day and journal about it or discuss it with a friend.

2. If you are not baptized, talk to your pastor about baptism. If you are, see what you can recall about it or ask others who were there what they remember.

3. Read the story of Jesus' baptism in Scripture.

2. MAKING THE BED: LITURGY, RITUAL, AND WHAT FORMS A LIFE

1. Do you make your bed? Why or why not? If you do, when do you do it?

2. Are there small, repetitive habits in your day that point you to a particular view of the "good life"? What are they?

3. Can you think of a daily practice or ritual that has formed or shaped you in a big or small way? Is there a practice or liturgy that has malformed you and may need to change?

4. How does your morning ritual or rhythm "imprint" you or your day?

5. Flannery O'Connor wrote that we must "push as hard as the age that pushes against you." How do you think practices and liturgies function in that challenge?

6. Do you think the way you worship in church affects your way of being-in-the-world in your ordinary day? If so, how?

7. Likewise, how do your daily, small "liturgies" affect your worship on Sunday?

8. The author says, "I need rituals that encourage me to embrace what is repetitive, ancient, and quiet." Do you agree or disagree that we need such rituals? What might that look like in your life?

9. How might you cultivate practices of stillness in your own life?

Suggested Practices:

1. As you make your bed, notice what you feel. What is tangible about the experience? Is there anything beautiful or peaceful about it?

2. Write down a repetitive, daily task in your life. As you perform this task, prayerfully ask God to show you the way it shapes you. Journal about it or discuss it with a friend.

3. Try to notice this week how you resist stillness and boredom. Carve out a few minutes of silence each day and invite God into that time.

4. Notice small moments of stillness in a day—waiting at a traffic light or for your coffee to brew. Embrace those moments by letting them remain empty and quiet.

5. If you have a smartphone, put it away for a morning, afternoon, or day and reflect on that experience.

3. BRUSHING TEETH: STANDING, KNEELING, BOWING, AND LIVING IN A BODY

1. Have you thought of the care of your body as part of your spiritual life and worship?

2. What experiences have shaped your view of the body and your relationship with your own body?

3. How do you think the incarnation—God's taking on a human body—impacts our worship and life in Christ?

4. In what ways has your body itself helped you or led you into worship?

5. The author writes, "If the church does not teach us what our bodies are for, our culture certainly will." What does our culture tell us about what our bodies are and what they are for?

6. The author compares the misuse or rejection of our bodies to denigrating a sacred object. Do you agree or disagree with this comparison? Why?

7. How does viewing the body as sacred impact our understanding of morality?

8. Does understanding your body as a place of worship affect the way you live in a body in an ordinary day? If so, how?

9. Do you experience seeing your reflection in the mirror as a time to embrace your freedom and belovedness in Christ? Why or why not?

10. How do Jesus' bodily resurrection and the eternal nature of our bodies impact how you think about body maintenance?

Suggested Practices:

1. As you look at your face in the mirror and brush your teeth this week, thank God for creating and loving your body.

2. Use your body in worship by kneeling, singing, or walking.

3. Write down one concrete way to care for your body. Reflect on or journal about the ways caring for your body impacts your life in Christ.

4. Notice the way you use your body in worship and what your church's liturgy communicates about human embodiment.

4. Losing Keys: Confession and the Truth About Ourselves

1. When small things go wrong in your day, how do you respond? What do you do? Give examples.

2. What does your response to inconveniences or "small" suffering reveal about your loves and fears? About your heart?

3. Is there anything in your life that, like the author, you feel a "right to be annoyed" about?

4. The author says that her theology of suffering is sometimes "too big" to touch her daily life. Have you ever experienced this? How?

5. Have you ever confessed sin aloud to another person? Why or why not? If so, what was that like?

6. What is your response to moments of sin or failure in your day? How might you meet God in those moments?

7. How is confessing sins with others different from confessing them privately? How is it related?

8. What would help you to believe in and rely on Christ's work and mercy when you encounter your weakness and sin in your day?

Suggested Practices:

1. Take note of your response when things go wrong in your day. Pray or journal about the fears and idols that those moments reveal in you.

2. The confession in the *Book of Common Prayer* states: "Most merciful God, we confess that we have sinned against you in thought, word, and deed, by what we have done, and by what we have left undone. We have not loved you with our whole heart; we have not loved our neighbors as ourselves. We are truly sorry and we humbly repent. For the sake of your Son, Jesus Christ, have mercy on us and forgive us, that we may delight in your will, and walk in your ways, to the glory of your Name. Amen." When you encounter sin in your day, specifically confess it to God and then pray this prayer or a similar one. Remind yourself aloud of God's mercy and forgiveness.

3. Have a time of confession with a friend or pastor. Ask them to remind you of Christ's forgiveness and mercy.

5. EATING LEFTOVERS: WORD, SACRAMENT, AND OVERLOOKED NOURISHMENT

1. The author describes her ideal for her table. What is yours?

2. How do our habits of eating, or of consumption and commerce more generally, form us?

3. What are some ways Christians can grapple with the ways our purchases contribute to social and environmental injustice?

4. What significance do you find in the fact that both Word and sacrament are related to food and eating?

5. The author describes how we can often have a "market-driven" spirituality, in which our personal experience becomes the centerpiece of our spiritual lives, instead of Word and sacrament. Do you agree or disagree? Can you cite examples of this "market-driven" mindset in the church or in your own life?

6. The author states, "With anonymity and ingratitude comes injustice." Do you agree? Why or why not?

7. Was there ever a time in your life when the Scriptures seemed dry or unappealing? How did you handle that?

8. What are the habits, liturgies, and rituals in church, culture, and daily lives that form us as mere consumers? As worshipers?

Suggested Practices:

1. Thank God for each meal you eat this week. If possible, find out where your food came from and pray for the people and place from which it came.

2. Read from the Gospels. Journal about places where you experience nourishment and the places where you struggle and feel like the Scriptures are stale or unappetizing.

3. In one day, notice how you are formed to value consumption, convenience, or self-fulfillment above all else. Notice whether gathered worship forms you differently than the broader culture of consumption.

4. Brainstorm ways of eating that are more connected to the land and to the people around you.

6. FIGHTING WITH MY HUSBAND: PASSING THE PEACE AND THE EVERYDAY WORK OF SHALOM

1. In what ways do you struggle to seek peace with those nearest you?

2. What is one way to seek shalom in your home, work, or small sphere of daily experience?

3. Do you ever separate big, "radical" acts of peacemaking from the daily grind? How does that separation look in your life?

4. How do you think the practice of passing the peace in church affects worship and theology?

5. The author writes, "I need to be reminded that my family and community are part of a larger mission. And yet I also need to remember that my small sphere, my ordinary day, matters to the mission." In what ways are you reminded that you are part of a larger mission?

6. How do you see your small sphere and ordinary days as part of the broader mission and work of God's redemption?

7. The author quotes Anne Lamott, who said, "Earth is Forgiveness School. You might as well start at the dinner table. That way, you can do this work in comfortable pants." How do you seek reconciliation or need it in your home or in your daily life?

Suggested Practices:

1. Seek peace in some way with those nearest you today. At the end of the day, ask God to bring his kingdom through the small acts of "peace passing" in your day.

2. Practice reconciliation this week by apologizing to someone you've wronged. Ask those closest to you how you can better love and live at peace with them.

3. Write down ways that you struggle to seek peace in your ordinary day. Ask God to show you the way of peace in those places of struggle.

4. Pray about how to be part of God's broader redemption of the world in your own life.

5. Spend time praying for peace in your home, neighborhood, city, state, country, and world.

7. CHECKING EMAIL: BLESSING AND SENDING

1. What tasks do you most enjoy? Least enjoy?

2. Do you find in yourself a "hierarchy of holiness" that privileges certain kinds of work over others? Or different activities in your own job?

3. The author writes, "There is no competition between the work we do as a people in gathered worship . . . and our vocations in the world. For believers, the two are intrinsically part of one another." How do you see your work life and your worship entwined? How do they influence and shape each other?

4. The author writes about "vocational holiness." How would approaching work as a craft and as a place of formation change the way you think about your work?

5. How does this view of holiness as a craft affect your understanding of growth in the Christian life?

6. The author discusses a "third way—neither frantic activity nor escape from the workaday world. . . . This third way is marked by freedom from compulsion and anxiety because it is rooted in benediction—God's blessing and love. But it also actively embraces God's mission in the world into which we are sent."

Do you feel like you have found a "third way" in your work life? Why or why not?

7. Do you struggle to find a way of working that is less anxious, on one hand, or does not escape from the world, on the other? If so, how?

8. How might your identity as one "blessed and sent" change your life and work in the world?

Suggested Practices:

1. Pray each morning that God would send you out to do the work he has given you to do.

2. Reflect on how a task in your daily work forms you. Journal about ways your work has grown you in repentance and dependence on God.

3. Prayerfully invite God to teach you to approach your work tasks as prayers. What would it mean to be in your work, yet on your knees?

4. Try to do a task you don't like without complaining.

5. If you sometimes work more than is healthy, avoid email or work tasks after hours this week and spend that time in rest.

8. SITTING IN TRAFFIC: LITURGICAL TIME AND AN UNHURRIED GOD

1. What are some times in your day or seasons in your life when you've had to wait?

2. What is waiting like for you—what do you feel as you wait?

3. The author quotes Hans Urs von Balthasar, who writes that sin is rooted in impatience. "Patience [is] the basic constituent of

Christianity." Do you agree with this view of the central role of patience in the Christian life? Why or why not?

4. The author tells a story about her friend, Jan, who says that there are gifts in waiting. What gifts have you received in the process of waiting? How have you grown?

5. Have you ever practiced the liturgical year? If so, how did you notice that practice forming or shaping you, your view of time, or your days?

6. How does the liturgical year act as counterformation to the culture?

7. If you have practiced liturgical time, how has it taught you to embrace waiting or to slow down?

8. What relationship do you see between waiting, hope, and celebration? How have you seen these related in your own life?

9. The author states, "Christians are marked not only by patience, but also by longing. We are oriented to our future hope, yet we do not try to escape from our present reality." How does orientation to the future impact how you think about your work, life, and relationships in an ordinary day?

Suggested Practices:

1. Notice your reaction to times where you are forced to wait this week. Reflect on what your response reveals about your view of time.

2. In the middle of a moment of waiting, stop and prayerfully reflect on how that moment sheds light on our life in the "already and not yet." Journal about that experience or discuss it with a friend.

3. Find out what liturgical season you're in and adopt practices to honor and celebrate that season. Read and learn about the church year.

4. Next time you're waiting (whether in line, waiting for an appointment, in traffic, etc.), try to limit distractions. Put away your smartphone and any work while waiting. Just simply wait. Notice your thoughts, emotions, and surroundings.

9. CALLING A FRIEND: CONGREGATION AND COMMUNITY

1. The author describes Christian community, saying, "We speak the good news to each other. And we become good news to each other." How have you experienced that in your life?

2. Does your church practice responsive reading or call and response in any way? If so, how does it form you and your congregation?

3. The author talks about how Western evangelicalism can devalue the church. Do you agree or disagree with that? Why?

4. John Calvin quotes Cyprian's famous dictum that "he can no longer have God for his Father, who has not the Church for his mother." Do you agree or disagree? Why?

5. How do you feel that Christian friendship and community differ from other kinds of community?

6. How have you dealt with sin and brokenness in the church?

7. How has Christ met you in and through the church?

8. Have you struggled to connect with those in the church? If so, how?

9. The author quotes Lesslie Newbigin, who said, "None of us can be made whole till we are made whole together." How does this reality affect your life and worship?

Suggested Practices:

1. Call or visit a friend. Pray together and tell him or her how God has used him or her in your life.

2. Attend church this week. If you know friends there, be sure to check in with them. If not, meet new people as you can.

3. If you don't know your pastor, meet with him or her. Ask him or her to tell you the vision and commitments of your local congregation and how you might plug in to the life of your church. Pray for your local church, your local church leaders, your denomination, and the global people of God.

4. Spend time reading, studying, and meditating on 1 Corinthians 12:12-27.

10. Drinking Tea: Sanctuary and Savoring

1. What are some ways that you experience pleasure, delight, beauty, and artistry?

2. How have you seen God's character through pleasure, delight, beauty, and artistry?

3. Is reveling in pleasure and beauty easy or difficult for you? Why?

4. The author writes that embracing pleasure takes *intentionality* and *practice*. Do you agree or disagree? Why?

5. What are some ways you've been intentional about making space and time for beauty, enjoyment, or delight?

6. How do you experience sensuous pleasure or beauty in worship? How does that shape you and your church?

7. Have you ever had a "pleasure of appreciation" change into a "pleasure of need"? How did that affect you and your worship?

8. What are some ways that we might practice both discernment and delight?

9. How does worshiping through your senses influence your relationship with pleasure and beauty?

10. How do you think beauty is part of the mission of the church?

Suggested Practices:

1. Set aside intentional time this week to do something you find lovely, pleasurable, or delightful.

2. Taste, smell, or look at something pleasing and beautiful. Journal about or discuss that experience of beauty and how it orients and shapes you.

3. Notice your senses in church. What do you see, smell, taste, hear, and feel? How does that lead you into worship or adoration?

11. Sleeping: Sabbath, Rest, and the Work of God

1. What is your nightly routine?

2. How do your nightly habits shape you?

3. What keeps you from sleep? What keeps you up at night?

4. What do your sleep patterns, struggles, or habits reveal about your loves, fears, commitments, and what you trust?

5. The author writes, "This is the message we receive from our culture: No limits. Nothing should stop you, slow you down, or limit your freedom." Where do you see resistance to limits in your culture and in yourself?

6. Do you ever think of death when you go to sleep? What do you think of the author's claim that sleep serves as a small, daily memento mori?

7. The author discusses how evangelicalism's activistic and achievement culture can produce a "culture of restlessness." Do you agree? Why or why not?

8. How are physical and spiritual rest related to each other?

9. Do you believe that God can sometimes work more in you as you sleep than when you are awake? Why or why not?

10. The author says, "The gift of rest comes to us through ritual and routine. Unearned and abundant, it comes in repetition, in the learning of a habit, in the liturgy of the day." How did you see this throughout the book?

Suggested Practices:

1. Think through your nightly liturgy. Make sure it is teaching you good habits of rest. Go to bed on time and get enough sleep. Reflect on or journal about how a week of good rest affects you spiritually and physically.

2. Talk to a family member or friend about the things that keep you from rest. Pray about them.

3. If you do not practice a weekly day of rest, do so this week. Reflect on how it affects you and your view of time, limits, your body, and God.

4. In church, notice the ways you are called into resting in God and in the community of believers, or how you are restless or striving to achieve some spiritual state. Invite God into your worship and ask him to teach you to rest in him.

notes

1 WAKING

[1]See Martin Marty's chapter in *How I Pray*, ed. Jim Castelli (New York: Ballantine Books, 1994), 89.

[2]Dorothy Bass, *Receiving the Day: Christian Practices for Opening the Gift of Time* (San Francisco: Jossey-Bass, 2000), 20.

[3]Marty, *How I Pray*, 89.

[4]Dallas Willard, *The Divine Conspiracy: Rediscovering Our Hidden Life in God* (New York: Harper Collins, 1998), 347-48. I am grateful to Fr. Kenny Benge for this reference.

[5]Donald Spoto, *Alfred Hitchcock: Fifty Years of His Motion Pictures* (New York: Anchor Books, 1992), 41.

[6]Annie Dillard, *The Writing Life* (New York: Harper & Row, 1989), 32.

2 MAKING THE BED

[1]*Book of Common Prayer*, 137. The *BCP* is citing Psalm 51 here.

[2]James K. A. Smith, *Desiring the Kingdom: Worship, Worldview, and Cultural Formation* (Grand Rapids: Baker, 2009), 55.

[3]Flannery O'Connor, *The Habit of Being: Letters of Flannery O'Connor*, ed. Sally Fitzgerald (New York: Farrar, Straus and Giroux, 1979), 229.

[4]Smith, *Desiring the Kingdom*, 25.

[5]Ibid., 63.

[6]Ibid., 211.

[7]Ibid., 84.

[8]Carolyn Johnson, "People Prefer Electric Shocks to Time Alone with Thoughts," *Boston Globe*, July 3, 2014, www.bostonglobe.com/news /science/2014/07/03/idle/J2LpEcTdZzLykRCTnZ80fL/story.html.

[9]Kathleen Norris, *Quotidian Mysteries: Laundry, Liturgy, and "Women's Work"* (Mahwah, NJ: Paulist Press, 1998), 35.

3 Brushing Teeth

[1]Macy Nulman, ed., *The Encyclopedia of Jewish Prayer: The Ashkenazic and Sephardic Rites* (Lanham: Rowman and Littlefield, 1996), 42.

[2]Matthew Lee Anderson, *Earthen Vessels: Why Our Bodies Matter to Our Faith* (Minneapolis: Bethany House, 2011), 211.

[3]Stanley Hauerwas, *Christian Existence Today: Essays on Church, World, and Living in Between* (Eugene, OR: Wipf & Stock, 1988), 106.

[4]These two paragraphs are adapted from Tish Harrison Warren, "At a Loss for Words: Finding Prayer Through Liturgy, Silence, and Embodiment," *The Well* (blog), September 20, 2010, http://thewell.intervarsity.org/spiritual -formation/loss-words-finding-prayer-through-liturgy-silence-and -embodiment.

4 Losing Keys

[1]C. S. Lewis, *Letters to Malcolm: Chiefly on Prayer* (New York: Harcourt, 2002), 91.

[2]Rod Dreher, "Everydayness," *The American Conservative* (blog), November 12, 2012, www.theamericanconservative.com/dreher/everydayness-wallace -stevens.

[3]Rich Mullins said this during a concert in Lufkin, Texas, in July 1997. The video footage can be seen at www.youtube.com/watch?v=ZNYtYRbH6aI.

[4]*Book of Common Prayer*, 360.

[5]Ibid.

5 Eating Leftovers

[1]Most Christians agree that baptism and Communion, or the Eucharist, are sacraments, sometimes called "dominically instituted" sacraments because Jesus explicitly institutes both the Lord's Supper and baptism. Roman Catholics, Orthodox, and some Protestants also include other rites of the church rooted either in apostolic practice, the order of creation, or the history of the church: Confirmation, Reconciliation, the Anointing of the Sick,

Marriage, and Holy Orders. Some Christians reject the terminology of *sacrament* and instead use the word *ordinance*.

[2]N. T. Wright, *Luke for Everyone* (Louisville, KY: Westminster John Knox, 2004), 262.

[3]Norman Wirzba, *Food & Faith: A Theology of Eating* (Cambridge: Cambridge University Press, 2011), 180.

[4]Jesus tells his disciples this in Luke 10:8, and it became Francis's advice to the Friars Minor. See Ivan Gobry, *Saint Francis of Assisi* (San Francisco: Ignatius, 2006), 182.

[5]Eugene H. Peterson, *A Long Obedience in the Same Direction: Discipleship in an Instant Society* (Downers Grove, IL: InterVarsity Press, 1980), 16.

[6]Harry Stout, *The Divine Dramatist: George Whitefield and the Rise of Modern Evangelicalism* (Grand Rapids: Eerdmans, 1991), 64-65.

[7]John Wolfe, *The Expansion of Evangelicalism: The Age of Wilberforce, More, Chalmer, and Finney* (Downers Grove, IL: InterVarsity Press, 2007), 116-17.

[8]C. S. Lewis, *The Last Battle* (New York: HarperCollins, 1955), 156-70.

[9]*Book of Common Prayer*, 365.

[10]Farm workers have the lowest family income of any wage earners in America: 61 percent of farm workers and their families live in poverty. Charles Thompson, "Introduction," in *The Human Cost of Food: Farmworkers' Lives, Labor, and Advocacy*, ed. Charles Thompson and Melinda Wiggins (Austin: University of Texas, 2002), 12.

[11]Ira Jackson, interview in *The Corporation*, special edition. Two Disk Set DVD (Disk Two). Directed by Mark Achbar and Jennifer Abbott (Big Picture Media Corporation, 2004).

[12]William Cavanaugh, *Being Consumed: Economics and Christian Desire* (Grand Rapids: Eerdmans, 2008), 95.

6 FIGHTING WITH MY HUSBAND

[1]Waterdeep, "I Know the Plans," *Sink or Swim*, © 1999 by Hey Ruth Records, Compact Disc.

[2]C. S. Lewis, *The Screwtape Letters* (New York: HarperCollins, 2001), 11.

[3]Ibid., 13.

[4]Dom Gregory Dix, *The Shape of the Liturgy* (New York: Harper & Row, 1945), 107.

[5]Ibid., 106.

[6]Ibid.

[7]Anne Lamott, Facebook status update, April 8, 2015.

7 CHECKING EMAIL

[1]*Book of Common Prayer*, 366.

[2]Examples of this are Redeemer Presbyterian's Center for Faith and Work, the New City Commons Vocation and the Common Good Project, Regent Seminary's marketplace theology concentration, and a spate of books in recent years by evangelicals on faith and work, such as Amy Sherman, *Kingdom Calling: Vocational Stewardship for the Common Good* (Downers Grove, IL: InterVarsity Press, 2011); Tim Keller (with Katherine Leary Alsdorf), *Every Good Endeavor: Connecting Your Work to God's Work* (New York: Dutton, 2012); and Katelyn Beaty, *A Woman's Place: A Christian Vision for Your Calling in the Office, the Home, and the World* (Brentwood, TN: Howard Books, 2016).

[3]See Michael Horton, *Ordinary: Sustainable Faith in a Restless World* (Grand Rapids: Zondervan, 2014), 197-98. This point about the popular role of vocation in the Reformation was helpfully discussed in my interview with Horton on the White Horse Inn, which can be heard here: www.whitehorseinn.org/blog /entry/2013-show-archive/2013/09/01/whi-1169-courage-in-the-ordinary.

[4]Keller, *Every Good Endeavor*, 5-6.

[5]See Andy Crouch, *Playing God: Redeeming the Gift of Power* (Downers Grove, IL: InterVarsity Press, 2014), 79-84.

[6]Steven Garber, *Visions of Vocation* (Downers Grove, IL: InterVarsity Press, 2014), 18.

[7]Gustaf Wingren, *Luther on Vocation*, trans. Carl C. Rasmussen (Eugene, OR: Wipf and Stock, 1957), 9, citing *Luther's Works* (St. Louis: Concordia; Philadelphia: Fortress, 1955–86; 2009–), 6:10. Many thanks to Dr. Gordon Isaac and Todd Hains for generously helping me track down source information.

[8]Eugene Peterson, *Under the Unpredictable Plant: An Exploration in Vocational Holiness* (Grand Rapids: Eerdmans, 1992).

[9]Garber, *Visions of Vocation*, 189.

[10]Arcade Fire, "Sprawl II (Mountains Beyond Mountains)," *The Suburbs*, © 2010 Merge Records.

[11]Keller, *Every Good Endeavor*, 67.

[12]Robert Banks and R. Paul Stevens, *The Complete Book of Everyday Christianity* (Downers Grove, IL: InterVarsity Press, 1997), 1128.

[13]B. B. Warfield, "The Religious Life of Theological Students," B. B. Warfield: The Life, Thought, and Works of Benjamin Breckinridge Warfield (1851–1921), accessed October 27, 2015, http://bbwarfield.com/works/sermons-and -addresses/the-religious-life-of-theological-students/.

[14]Ibid.

[15]Ibid.

[16]Brother Lawrence, *The Practice of the Presence of God* (Grand Rapids: Spire Books, 1967), 30.

[17]*Book of Common Prayer*, 366.

8 Sitting in Traffic

[1]Jonathan Swift, *Gulliver's Travels* (New York: E. P. Dutton, 1912), 26.

[2]Hans Urs von Balthasar, *A Theology of History* (San Francisco: Ignatius, 1994), 36-37.

[3]Some of the material in this section first appeared in Tish Harrison Warren, "How the Liturgical Calendar Keeps Me Sane," *The Well* (blog), November 27, 2013, http://thewell.intervarsity.org/blog/how-liturgical-calendar-keeps -me-sane.

[4]Dorothy Bass, *Receiving the Day: Christian Practices for Opening the Gift of Time* (San Francisco: Jossey-Bass, 2000), 3.

[5]*Book of Common Prayer*, 501, 281.

[6]James K. A. Smith, *Desiring the Kingdom: Worship, Worldview, and Cultural Formation* (Grand Rapids: Baker, 2009), 200.

[7]This section first appeared in Tish Harrison Warren, "Waiting: Ache and the Gift in Between," *The Well* (blog), July 31, 2013, http://thewell.intervarsity .org/blog/waiting.

[8]Robert Louis Wilken, *The Spirit of Early Christian Thought: Seeking the Face of God* (New Haven: Yale University Press, 2005), 284.

[9]Smith, *Desiring the Kingdom*, 158.

9 Calling a Friend

[1]Madeleine L'Engle, *A Circle of Quiet* (New York: Farrar, Strauss and Giroux, 1972), 26.

[2]This is a quote from an email exchange between Rev. Canon Mary Hays and me on October 2, 2015. I am deeply grateful for her insight and wisdom—on this and so many other things.

[3]Cyprian, *On the Unity of the Church 6, Ante-Nicene Fathers* vol. 5, ed. Alexander Roberts and James Donaldson (Peabody, MA: Hendrickson Publishers, 1994), 423; Calvin, *Institutes of the Christian Religion* 4.1.1. See also Tish Harrison Warren, "The Church Is Your Mom," *Her.meneutics* (blog), May 21, 2015, www.christianitytoday.com/women/2015/may/church-is-your-mom.html.

[4]Our former priest, Thomas McKenzie, shares this in his book *The Anglican Way: A Guidebook* (Nashville: Colony Catherine, 2014), 202.

[5]Donald Miller, "Why I Don't Go to Church Very Often, a Follow Up Blog," *Storyline* (blog), accessed October 27, 2015, http://storylineblog.com/2014/02/05/why-i-dont-go-to-church-very-often-a-follow-up-blog.

[6]Michael Ramsey, *Glory Descending: Michael Ramsey and His Writings*, ed. Douglas Dales et al. (Grand Rapids: Eerdmans, 2005), 102.

[7]Flannery O'Connor, *The Habit of Being: Letters of Flannery O'Connor*, ed. Sally Fitzgerald (New York: Farrar, Straus and Giroux, 1979), 90.

[8]Ramsey, *Glory Descending*, 100.

[9]Lesslie Newbigin, *The Household of God: Lectures on the Nature of the Church* (Eugene, OR: Wipf & Stock, 2008), 147.

10 DRINKING TEA

[1]C. S. Lewis, *The Screwtape Letters* (New York: HarperCollins, 2001), 64.

[2]Ibid., 66.

[3]H. L. Mencken, *A Mencken Chrestomathy: His Own Selection of His Choicest Writing* (New York: Alfred A. Knopf, 1949), 624.

[4]Ben Witherington III, *Work: A Kingdom Perspective on Labor* (Grand Rapids: Eerdmans, 2011), 111.

[5]Francis Bremer, *Puritanism: A Very Short Introduction* (New York: Oxford University Press, 2009), 57-58.

[6]Ibid., 52-53.

[7]G. K. Chesterton, *Orthodoxy* (New York: John Lane Co., 1909), 109.

[8]My thanks to Monique Ingalls for speaking with me about forms of non-Western worship music and the catechetical function of music throughout the history of the church as I worked on this chapter.

[9]James K. A. Smith, *Desiring the Kingdom: Worship, Worldview, and Cultural Formation* (Grand Rapids: Baker, 2009), 25.

[10]C. S. Lewis, *Letters to Malcolm: Chiefly on Prayer* (New York: Harcourt, 2002), 88.

[11]Ibid., 89-90.

[12]Ibid.

[13]Annie Dillard et al., "The Meaning of Life, The Big Picture," *Life Magazine*, December 1988, www.maryellenmark.com/text/magazines/life/905W -000-037.html. Thank you to Marcia Bosscher for this reference.

[14]This story appears in Tish Harrison Warren, "Giving Up and Taking Up: What We Do (and Don't Do) When We Keep Lent," *The Well* (blog), February 12, 2013, https://thewell.intervarsity.org/spiritual-formation/giving -and-taking-what-we-do-and-dont-do-when-we-keep-lent.

[15]Walter Wangerin, *The Book of Sorrows* (Grand Rapids: Zondervan, 1985), 303-4.

[16]Carolyn Arends, "Worship con Queso," *Christianity Today*, August 29, 2013, www.christianitytoday.com/ct/2013/september/worship-con-queso.html.

[17]Ibid.

[18]Neil Postman, *Amusing Ourselves to Death: Public Discourse in the Age of Show Business* (New York: Penguin, 1985).

[19]Lewis, *Letters to Malcolm*, 91.

[20]Dostoevsky puts this line in the mouth of his protagonist Prince Myshkin in *The Idiot*. Fyodor Dostoevsky, *The Idiot*, trans. Frederick Wishaw (London: Vizetelly & Co., 1887), 257.

[21]Czesław Miłosz, "One More Day," in *The Collected Poems, 1931–1987* (New York: Ecco Press, 1998), 407.

11 SLEEPING

[1]"Why a Regular Bedtime Is Important for Children," *Morning Edition*, KUT Austin Public Radio, December 16, 2013, http://www.npr.org/2013/12 /16/251462015/why-a-regular-bedtime-is-important-for-children.

[2]*Book of Common Prayer*, 134.

[3]Ibid.

[4]Center for Disease Control and Prevention, "Insufficient Sleep Is a Public Health Problem," September 3, 2015, www.cdc.gov/features/dssleep. Debra Goldschmidt, "The Great American Sleep Recession," CNN, February 18, 2015, www.cnn.com/2015/02/18/health/great-sleep-recession.

[5]Wendell Berry, *Life Is a Miracle: An Essay Against Modern Superstition* (Berkeley: Counterpoint, 2001), 55.

[6]*Book of Common Prayer*, 134.

[7] Rod Dreher, "Harmony, Communion, Incarnation," *The American Conservative* (blog), June 23, 2015, www.theamericanconservative.com/dreher /harmony-communion-incarnation-laudato-si-pope-francis/.

[8] "Fear of Sleep," *This American Life*, WBEZ Chicago Public Radio, August 8, 2008, www.thisamericanlife.org/radio-archives/episode/361/fear-of-sleep.

[9] Saint Benedict, *The Rule of Saint Benedict*, trans. Bruce Venarde (Cambridge: Harvard University Press, 2011), 35.

[10] *Book of Common Prayer*, 265.

[11] Quoted in Michael Horton, "Ordinary: The New Radical?," *Key Life* (blog), October 24, 2014, www.keylife.org/articles/ordinary-the-new-radical -michael-horton.

[12] David Bebbington, *Evangelicalism in Modern Britain: A History from the 1730s to the 1980s* (Grand Rapids: Baker, 1989), 11.

[13] Mark Galli, *Beyond Smells and Bells: The Wonder and Power of Christian Liturgy* (Brewster, MA: Paraclete Press, 2008), 80.

[14] Eugene Peterson, *Working the Angles: The Shape of Pastoral Integrity* (Grand Rapids: Eerdmans, 1987), 68.

[15] Dorothy Bass, *Receiving the Day: Christian Practices for Opening the Gift of Time* (San Francisco: Jossey-Bass, 2000), 18.

[16] John Baillie, "The Theology of Sleep," in *Christian Devotion: Addresses by John Baillie* (Oxford: Oxford University Press, 1962), 103.

[17] Ibid.

[18] This paragraph and parts of the next two are from Tish Harrison Warren, "Spiritual Direction: Get More Sleep," *The Well* (blog), October 29, 2013, http://thewell.intervarsity.org/blog/spiritual-direction-get-more-sleep.

formatio
TRADITION. EXPERIENCE.
TRANSFORMATION.

Formatio books from InterVarsity Press follow the rich tradition of the church in the journey of spiritual formation. These books are not merely about being informed, but about being transformed by Christ and conformed to his image. Formatio stands in InterVarsity Press's evangelical publishing tradition by integrating God's Word with spiritual practice and by prompting readers to move from inward change to outward witness. InterVarsity Press uses the chambered nautilus for Formatio, a symbol of spiritual formation because of its continual spiral journey outward as it moves from its center. We believe that each of us is made with a deep desire to be in God's presence. Formatio books help us to fulfill our deepest desires and to become our true selves in light of God's grace.